Ingrid Belčáková, László Miklós, Anna Špinerová, Andrea Diviaková, Erika Kočická, Eliška Belaňová

SPECTRUM SLOVAKIA Series
Volume 16

Landscape considerations in spatial planning

VEDA

PETER LANG

Bibliographic Information published by the Deutsche Nationalbibliothek
The Deutsche Nationalbibliothek lists this publication in the Deutsche Nationalbibliografie; detailed bibliographic data is available in the internet at http://dnb.d-nb.de.

Authors:
Ingrid Belčáková (Chapters 1-3)
László Miklós (Chapters 1-2)
Anna Špinerová (Chapter2)
Andrea Diviaková (Chapter 3)
Erika Kočická (Chapter 3)
Eliška Belaňová (Chapter 3)

Cover Photo: Lucia Belčáková

UNESCO Department for Ecological Awareness and Sustainable Development, Faculty of Ecology and Environmental Sciences, Technical University in Zvolen, Slovakia

ISSN 2195-1845
ISBN 978-3-631-74971-5
Ebook: 978-3-631-78300-9
ePub: 978-3-631-78301-6
MOBI: 978-3-631-78302-3
ISBN 978-80-224-1695-5

This publication has been peer reviewed.

www.peterlang.com
www.veda.sav.sk

Contents

Acknowledgements

The authors are grateful to the reviewers for their assistance and constructive and valuable suggestions. The publishing of the book was supported by the KEGA cultural and educational grant agency, project no. 13TUZ-4/2016 titled "The Didactic Support of the Study Programme "Environmental Management" in English Language.

List of illustrations

Figures

Tables

Foreword

The landscape is a vital spatial and material frame for our natural and man-made environment and is considered by many stakeholders to be one of the most important aspect of a healthy, enjoyable life. During the last several decades, we have witnessed its vulnerability in the face of economic growth and social change. Man and his activities significantly affect the landscape, its structure, components, etc. Human activities in the landscape are not always in harmony with its resources and potential. This non-compliance is the foundation of the emergence of environmental problems.

Often, we have failed adequately to predict, recognise or deal with the impact of new developments. The result has been serious erosion of the character and quality of many of our urban and rural landscapes.

In planning for future prosperity, more effort must be put into safeguarding the quality of the environment, not only for our own health and well-being, but also for the sake of future generations. This implies a strong need to integrate issues of landscape management into the development process.

Sustainable spatial development is a fast-moving issue all over the world. New approaches and applications are emerging all the time. Despite recent progress, there is still much to do to make the management of landscape effective and more widely applied.

This book is intended to deal primarily with the current trends in the theory of integration of landscape aspects in spatial planning and development processes. Ultimately, the need for integrating planning, particularly land use planning, landscape planning and impact assessment, is also a part of discussion.

In this book, landscape considerations practice in European countries is covered, with a special focus on Slovakia. The aim has been to draw together information about landscape decision-making approaches and cases that illustrate current practice and lessons from experience. This provides baseline material for landscape academic forum and members of the public to let them know what they should request. We hope that this will also be of wider interest and help to many professions in spatial development making: planners, designers, architects, engineers and others.

The first part sets landscape considerations in spatial planning in its European context. It presents the philosophy and common principles which should underline sustainable spatial planning and/or spatial development processes. It sets out the current philosophy towards the sustainable land use and spatial development.

Part 2 represents the core of the book and it deals with sustainable spatial development tools and practice in different areas of application. Spatial and/or land use planning definitely represents one of the most comprehensive planning tools where landscape assessment has already been applied for last several decades. That is why authors have been trying to make an overview of the state of art in this field based on own experience and the international know how. Best practices and experience that are described in this part have resulted from an analytical survey of a number of case studies. Finally, a special attention is paid to a possible identification of what are the remaining most pressing needs in this field and other suggestions that have been shared during their own practice. The Strategic Environmental Assessment (SEA) part is focused on pointing out the "added value" and potential benefits of linking environmental assessment processes with landscape planning instruments, with a special accent to landscape ecological methods and techniques that can take place.

A special attention is given to Landscape-Ecological Planning methods and techniques to be applied in environmental assessment procedures. Furthermore, it gives a summary of practical experience in this field based on available reference as well as on a number of published case studies and on personal experience. They are followed by the conclusions and proposals for future developments and future research.

Coverage in case studies part (Part 3) varies in extent and depth reflecting available information.

The review presented in this book is intended to provide a sourcebook and reference guide to key trends and issues of sustainable spatial development, and to the different approaches being used in European countries. This effort has meant that the book is both practice-oriented and as up-to-date as possible.

1
Background

Ingrid Belčáková, László Miklós

1.1 The context of landscape considerations in spatial planning processes

Land use is determined on one side by the attributes of natural components, which represent a specific offer for a human. On the other side, land use is determined by requirements, demands, capacities and overall possibilities for the society. The requirements, demands as well as the overall possibilities change in the course of time (change of human conditions, change of priorities, change of ownership, change in technologies, etc.). What was once a luxurious commodity became an essential one. The change in the demands and requirements of the human society cyclically appears in changed forms and intensity of landscape use. On the other side, the changes can be caused by the repercussion of the natural environment against a specific land use, if it becomes unsustainable; e.g. improper land use can cause or potentially accelerate the natural risks and hazards, which take part in the change of landscape structure and land use. Often, changes within the society that potentially affect landscape are much faster and variable in comparison with the sustained natural process of landscape development (Izakovičová, 2012).

Many European countries have faced substantial socio-economic changes in the recent period, which are also reflected in the environmental area. Political regimes changed in some European countries from the central socialist planning policy to the market-driven economy; markets opened and established contacts not only in the European but also the world context. Accession of new member states to the European Union has increased the rate of advancing world globalisation.

These structural changes had also negative impact on land use and land cover. Significant pressures of investors, developers and various lobbyist groups on land use exist and are driven by various motifs such as the construction of technology parks, logistic centres or development of recreational activities. Technical elements are often inappropriately located in the landscape and the trend is increasing in the majority of the European countries. Migration of population - partly migration of the rural population to the urban area in search of more work opportunities or contrariwise, immigration of urban population into rural area preferring the better environment - will also find reflection in the change of landscape use.

There has also been a major change in the structure of agriculture like abandoned agricultural land and different structure of crops, decreased rate of agricultural production, increasing pressure on occupation of agricultural land and other natural resources due to the aggressive promotion of certain investment projects, but also increasing of pressure on natural resources connected with the implementation of environmental measurements, etc. The negative impact of abandoned fields manifests in the diminishing landscape biodiversity, desertification of land, decrease of native plant and animal species, increasing mono-cultures in plant production, increase of synantropic species, high yielding cattle in livestock production, falling groundwater levels and increasing load on the regional water regime, heavier pollution impact on ecological systems, as well as the progressive soil compaction, erosion, salinisation, etc. (Miklós, Izakovičová 2007; Wiggering et al., 2007). Changes in landscape structure and substantial antropisation are the principal causes of climate change, which besides the changes in natural ecosystems and biodiversity causes more intensive natural risks and hazards as floods, droughts, etc. The base for the elimination of these problems is *the implementation of sustainable land use management*.

Several instruments have been designed to assist strategic decision-making, including spatial planning, in improving the quality of policies, plans and programmes in its capacity to contribute towards sustainable development, and, in this context, with considerations of landscape impacts resulting from strategic decisions. To successfully fulfil this challenge spatial planning and development must ensure full consideration of landscape and/or other environmental issues through a broad, holistic and integrative way, which should be inherent to the nature of land-use planning, but where practice evidently shows it is still lagging behind.

Spatial planning usually covers a wider system of spatially relevant planning instruments and it is closely related to optimal and efficient distribution (allocation) of various development proposals and activities in territories and in space (Belčáková, 1995; Belčáková and Finka, 2000; Belčáková, 2001). Regarding *sustainability* as the new development concept, the coordination of individual (sectoral) proposals in order to reach or at least to come close to sustainable development is an obvious challenge. In this respect, several landscape planning and assessment processes can play an important and immutable role.

With regard to the new challenges that development faces to date (economic globalisation, devolution of decision-making power to lower levels of government, urbanisation processes, deterioration of the environment) and in view of the new development paradigms (sustainable development, local agenda 21, public participation), spatial planning and development processes have to adopt the role of anticipating development, proposing alternatives and measures, and co-ordinating sector activities.

Environmental, social and economic aspects should be integrated during the process of spatial planning and the appropriate instruments can reach this. These are mostly represented by *landscape planning and Strategic Environmental Assessment.*

Landscape plan is in many European countries an essential tool of sustainable land use because it regulates socio-economic development with natural, human, cultural and historical potential of landscape (see Tab. 1). Decision-making process of the landscape-ecological optimal utilisation of the territory in the landscape plan is based on matching the offer, which is represented by the resources in the region, and demand which is represented by the community needs of growth and development. The discrepancy between offer and demand (not respecting the properties of landscape resources) is the determining factor of formation of not only environmental but also human problems (Izakovičová, 2012; Belčáková, 2012).

Tab. 1: Examples of landscape planning systems

Country	Legislation	Objectives	Contents
Germany	Federal Nature Conservation Act 2004 (comprehensive landscape plans at all planning levels)	- Sustained availability of the natural resources for human use - Integration of considerations of nature and landscape into decision-making (especially in terms of spatial planning)	- Existing and anticipated status of nature and landscape - Principles of nature conservation and landscape management - Assessment and evaluation of the existing and anticipated status of nature and landscapes, possible conflicts - Measures for avoiding, reducing or eliminating adverse effects on nature and landscapes - Measures for protecting, managing and developing certain parts or components of nature and landscape

Slovakia	Act on Town and Country Planning and Building Code (comprehensive landscape plans at regional and local levels)	- Optimal spatial arrangement of human activities based on landscape ecological conditions	- Landscape ecological analysis of landscape elements and factors - Syntheses of landscape ecological characteristics - Interpretation of landscape conditions - Ecological optimisation of land use
Scotland	No formal requirements (landscape character assessment – guidance for England and Scotland)	- Landscape character assessment as a reference point in policy, plan and programme formulation - To inform decision-making about change and development, so they are consistent with landscape objectives	- Digital landscape character types database - Provides a baseline against which change can be monitored and to inform decision-making - Identification of critical areas - Visualisation of the results for use in potential management regimes - Recommendations regarding mitigation and design considerations
Sweden	No formal requirements (ecological landscape plans)	- Sustained availability of the natural resources	- Existing and anticipated status of natural resources and landscape - Principles of nature conservation and landscape management including health aspects - Assessment and evaluation of the existing and anticipated status of nature and landscapes, possible conflicts - Measures for avoiding, reducing or eliminating adverse effects on nature and landscapes - Measures for protecting, managing and developing certain parts or components of nature and landscape - Implementation of health aspects

Source: Adapted from Belčáková, 2012

At the moment, major projects likely to have an impact on the environment must be assessed by *environmental impact assessment (EIA) process.* However, this assessment takes place at a stage when options for significant change are often limited. Decisions on the site of a project, or on the choice of alternatives may already have been taken in the context of plans for a whole sector or geographical area. In this context, the assessment of "high level or strategic activities", which is usually called *Strategic Environmental Assessment (SEA)*, can plug this gap and it is inevitable to be part of each spatial system in spatial planning processes in order to search for the common basis of the topic of integration. It has been seen as an appropriate instrument in order to integrate environmental, social and economic issues in spatial planning.

EIA and SEA are *legislated in most countries.* After years of implementation, its quality, effectiveness and efficiency is generally recognised. In Europe, the *European Union Directives* are of key importance for both processes. EIA and SEA is also an important step forward in European environmental law since the SEA Directive has been adopted (Directive 2001/42/EC). It requires the environmental effects of a broad range of plans and programmes to be assessed while plans are actually being developed, and in due course adopted (see Tab. 2).

Directive 2001/42/EC of the European Parliament and of the Council on the assessment of the effects of certain plans and programmes on the environment of 27 June 2001 (the "SEA Directive") provides for the compulsory assessment of plans and programmes, which predetermine the framework for future permitting of specific development projects in the field of agriculture, forestry, fisheries, water management, energy, industry, transport, waste management, telecommunications, tourism, and spatial planning, and which affect protected areas under NATURA 2000 (EC, 2001). The mandatory assessment applies to all plans and programmes with significant effect on the environment, regardless of the hierarchical level of public administration (national, regional, local) including plans and programmes co-financed by the European Community.

Directive 2014/52/EU of the European Parliament and the Council on the assessment of the effects of certain public and private projects on the environment (codified) of 16 April 2014, amending the Directive 2011/92/EU on the assessment of the effects of certain public and private projects on the environment (the "EIA Directive"), refers to the assessment of the effects of those public and private projects which are likely to have significant effect on the environment (EC, 2014). Projects are understood as execution of construction works or other equipment, plans and interventions into the natural environment and the landscape, including those involving the extraction of mineral resources in accordance with Annexes 1 and 2 of the Directive.

Both the above-mentioned formal provisions set out the basic principles and assessment principles, areas of application, including the proposal of individual procedural steps, which – as a standard – include detailed description of the proposed plan, programme or investment project, the current state of the environment, identification and assessment of potential impact, design of compensation measures and presentation of results of the assessment process.

The UN ECE Convention E/EEC/1250 on impact assessment in a transboundary context of 25 February 1991 (Espoo Convention) and the UN ECE Convention on Access to Information, Public Participation in Decision-making and Access to Justice in Environmental matters of 25 June 1998 (Aarhus Convention) is yet another essential international formal requirement for environmental impact assessment. The Protocol on Strategic Environmental Assessment to the UNECE Convention on Environmental Impact Assessment in a Transboundary Context (SEA Protocol) is also imperative for implementation and application of the SEA. Further key conventions include the Convention on biological diversity, the Convention on the Conservation of Migratory Species of Wild Animals (Bonn Convention), the Convention on the Conservation of European Wildlife and Natural Habitats (Bern Convention), the Convention on the Conservation of European nature and the natural habitats of Europe, the Convention on Wetlands of International Importance especially as Waterfowl Habitat (Ramsar Convention), the Convention on the protection of the World Cultural and Natural Heritage (UNESCO), the Convention on international trade in endangered species of wild fauna and flora (Washington Convention – CITES), the European Landscape Convention, and others.

SEA is inevitable to be a control instrument also for spatial planning processes. It aims to address the issue of integration of ecological, economic and social issues in spatial planning. The most important function of SEA in spatial planning is its contribution to a stronger ecological orientation. On one hand, SEA directly joins the process of planning and decision-making and on the other hand, it can meet those impacts that interfere above the framework of the actual decision-making process in land-use planning.

SEA has been seen in various forms, one being that it represents an important step towards integrated decision-making, promoting sustainable development by assessing the strengths, weaknesses and therefore

Tab. 2: SEA requirements in spatial/land-use planning in EU member states before SEA Directive transposition

Country	Spatial/land-use planning decision-making levels	Formal requirements (separate EIA/SEA legislation or within planning legal instruments)	Scope of application in spatial/land-use planning	SEA approach	Changes after SEA Directive transposition
Austria	National, state (lander), district/regional, municipal	No legal requirement,	Local land-use plans, supra-local land-use plans	EIA-based	Amendment to land-use planning sector
Belgium	National, regional, local	No explicit environmental evaluation,	To some extent, Regional land-use plans in Brussels and Flanders region	EIA-based	Amendment to existing EIA regulation – EIA and SEA Decree in Flanders
Bulgaria	National, regional, local	EIA Regulation No.1(1995)	National development programmes, all level land-use plans	EIA-based	Amendment to existing EIA legislation
Cyprus	National, regional, local	No legal requirement at all			Explicit SEA legislation – Law No. 102 (I) 2005
Czech Rep.	National, regional, local	Provisions for some form of SEA in EIA Act No 244/92	Regional and local land-use plans, national development plan	EIA-based	Amendment to existing EIA regulation – EIA Act No. 100/2001 Coll., different procedure for SEA of land-use plans, SEA reflection in Law on Construction and Land Use Planning is under preparation
Denmark	National, regional / county, municipal	Some provisions in Prime Minister's Office Circular since 1997, voluntary basis since 1990	Regional and municipal land-use planning documentation, local plans, national plan statements	EIA-based	Explicit SEA legislation – Act on Environmental Assessment of Plans and Programmes
Estonia	National, regional, local	Provisions for some form of SEA in the Law on EIA and Environmental Audit	Local plans, national development plans or programmes	EIA-based	Amendment to existing EIA regulation – Environmental Impact Assessment and Environmental management System Act

Finland	National, regional, local	Building and Planning Act, EIA Act	Land-use plans at all decision-making levels	EIA-based	Explicit SEA legislation and also within land-use planning regulations – Act and Decree on the assessment of the Impacts of the Authorities, Plans, Programmes and Policies on the Environment, Land Use and Building Act and Decree
France	National, regional, local	Decision of the French Parliament	Certain land-use plans	EIA-based	Amendment to environment code – one part specifically relates to spatial planning
Germany	Federal, state, regional (county), local	Formal landscape planning system – Federal Environmental protection Act, 1976	Local land-use plans, local and regional landscape plans and programmes, state development plans,	EIA-based + landscape planning approach	Amendment to existing EIA regulation – Act for Introducing SEA, also Federal Spatial Planning Act, Federal Construction Law
Greece	National, regional	No SEA legislation, but "EIA" of small scale land-use plans took place	Small scale land-use plans	EIA-based	No SEA legislation,
Hungary	National, county, municipal	Environment Act (1995)	Regional development plans	EIA-based	Amendment of EIA Act in 2004 and Government Decree on the Environmental Assessment of Certain Plans and Programmes in 2005
Ireland	National, local	Government decision of 1978 No formal procedure	National land-use plans, little experience with Master plans, local area plans	EIA-based	Explicit SEA legislation – Environmental Assessment of Certain Plans and Programmes Regulations 2004, Planning and Development (SEA) Regulations 2004

Italy	National, regional, local	Some formal SEA requirements, regional planning legislation (e.g. Regional Planning Law No.20/20	Regional spatial plans	EIA-based approach	Amendment to environment code – Act on Environmental matters, April 2006
Latvia	National, regional, local	Provisions for some form of SEA in EIA Law	Regional and local plans, national development plans		Amendment to existing EIA regulation – EIA Act on 26 February 2004
Lithuania	National, regional, local	Provisions for some form of SEA in EIA Law (1996) and territorial planning law of 1995	County comprehensive plans, district comprehensive plans, national development plans	EIA-pproach	Amendment to environment code – Law on Environmental protection of the Republic of Lithuania, Law on Territorial Planning
Luxembourg	National, regional, local	No SEA legislation			No SEA legislation
Malta	National, regional, local	No SEA legislation	Regional development plans	EIA-approach	Explicit SEA legislation
Netherlands	National, regional, local	No SEA legislation, but "EIA" of small scale land-use plans took place, several informal SEAs	Local land-use plans	EIA-based and integrated	Amendment to environment code – Environmental Management Act, revised in July 2006
Poland	National, regional, local	Provisions for some form of SEA in the Law on Access to Information on the Environment, Its Protection and EIA (2002)	Regional and local land-use plans, national development plans	EIA-based	Amendment to existing EIA regulation / Act on Access to Information about the Environment and its Protection and on the Environmental Impact Assessment, and also Environmental protection Law
Portugal	National, regional, local	Non-standard approach to plan making, sea not applied	Regional and local land-use planning and spatial programmes submitted to EU Structural Funds	EIA- and policy-based	SEA legislation is still under preparation

Romania	National, regional, local	Environmental protection Law No.137/1995	All land-use plans	EIA-based	Law on urban and territorial planning + Government Ordinance (2004)
Slovakia	National, regional, local	Provisions for some form of SEA in EIA Act No.127/1994, amended 2000)	Regional and local land-use plans, national development plan	EIA-based	Amendment to existing EIA regulation / New Act No.24/2006
Slovenia	National, regional, local	Provisions for some form of SEA in Environmental Protection Act (1993)	Regional and local land-use plans, national development plan	EIA-based	Environmental Protection Act
Spain	National, regional, local	Part of EIA legislation	Regional land-use plans		Explicit SEA legislation / SEA law of April 2006
Sweden	Regional, local	National Resources Management Act	Local land-use plans – mostly at municipal level	Integrated land-use planning	Amendment to environment code, 2004
UK	National, regional, subregional, local	No statutory form of SEA, various non-statutory measures at national level	Structure plans, local land-use plans	Sustain-ability appraisal-policy-based	Environmental assessment of Plans and Programmes Regula-tions 2004 (England and Wales – Planning and Compulsory Purchase Act of 2004 Scotland – Environment Assessment (Scot-land) Bill)

Source: Belčáková, 2016

the potential of environmental resources to support development (CSIR, 1996). It is also seen as providing "an entry point to the appraisal of sustainable development by ensuring that environmental considerations are addressed at the same level and at the same time as social and economic issues in policy making" (DETR, 1998).

1.2 Participatory planning as a background philosophy towards sustainable spatial development

Public involvement in planning and decision-making on the landscape as part of the environmental decision-making is particularly important in terms of its sustainable development and the preservation of identity. Social participation and co-operation with the public is the basis for a successful management system for the landscape, without which its success would be greatly reduced. It forms the basis for the effectiveness of spatially relevant planning processes as well as for programmes of conservation, creation and landscape management.

Locals can explain the values and the nature of the landscape and its overall environment, to identify the most important conflicts and issues in its territory and also to express what kind of landscape they require in the future and how they want to change it. In this context it often refers to the target quality of landscape according to the philosophy of the European Landscape Convention. The landscape quality objectives should constitute the outcome of the proposed planning objectives and activities in the landscape to be undertaken in the spirit of participatory planning.

Social participation as one of the tools of sustainable territorial development is a process in which the decision-making, management and spatial development at all hierarchical levels (municipality, region and the entire country) integrate aspects of all stakeholders – individuals, public, governmental and non-governmental organisations (NGOs), local self-government; public administration and others. Participation of citizens in sustainable spatial development depends on enabling broad public participation in the management with the support of the relevant legal system as a tool for practical implementation of public participation.

In the process of social participation, the public is every person or a group of people having a personal interest in solving a particular problem, or wanting to comment on it. This term is filled for content always depending on specific conditions. Part of the public in this regard can be individuals; groups of citizens; groups of entrepreneurs; public interest groups; industrial, commercial, agricultural, medical and other organizations; local clubs and associations; NGOs; environmental movements; civic associations and civic initiatives, i.e. all those who may be affected or involved in planning, assessment and decision-making on a planned activity or a strategic intent.

The public cannot be regarded as an unchanging entity. Rather we can say that it is a constantly changing set of people, who are grouped based on a common understanding of interest. It is therefore necessary to accept that there are different types of the public and public with different number of its members. The basic trend is that the number of its members is increasing in parallel with a growth of interest and involvement on the issue. Citizens are involved and participate when they feel that the whole issue seriously affects them. They do not participate if they believe that it does not affect them, or when the extent and nature of the issue gives rise to a feeling that it cannot be influenced.

When designing procedures for public participation, it is very useful to consider two fundamentally different positions of the public, in which it acts as a partner in planning, assessment and decision-making. In principle, it is possible to allocate two semantically equivalent positions of the public – as a *vehicle for information* and as a *recipient of information* and commenting entity (Belčáková and Petríková, 2003).

In many cases, despite sufficient public information, the public remains in the position of a "silent majority". In fact, everyone chooses his/her own time, when he/she wishes to participate, and whether he/she wants to be in that period part of the voicing minority or of the silent majority. Silent majority is always a potential group of voicing minority, which is just not involved at this point and can easily revise its reasons for non-participation in the decision-making as not substantial or temporary. This, however, only if approached in a sensitive way and patiently informed, with all diligence.

Although the public includes every citizen, it is not always a participating citizen. In the process of public participation it never reaches the entire public. Therefore it is justified to talk about involving the public, or about participating public. The process of activation of a citizen towards the public concerned has in a sense its national specificities resulting from the maturity of democracy and respecting the principle of citizenship in this or that State (Belčáková and Petríková, 2003).

The basic principles of social participation in the decision-making and planning process clearly include the *aspect of democracy*, allowing a broad public including other entities. The opinions and comments of the public should be respected at all stages of the assessment, planning and decision-making processes.

Another significant principle of social participation is the aspect of public involvement. Public involvement is a multifaceted communication that follows the way of accepting public as an immediate and equal entity, with this it is necessary to have a dialogue and to take its opinions or views. As further referred to by the already mentioned authors, this is a two-way communication:

- In the top-down approach, these are promoters of development projects and strategic intents.
- In the bottom-up approach, these are citizens, civic associations and initiatives, entering the process of evaluation, planning and decision-making.

Effective model of public participation should be designed in a way to achieve the following objectives:

- Mapping geographic, cultural and historical, social and demographic realities of the site under assessment.
- Identifying public interests, social needs and values.
- Collecting economic, environmental and social information from the public.
- Informing the public about alternative solutions in the plans.
- Developing partnership contacts between public, local government, investors, interest groups and NGOs.
- Developing and maintaining mutual trust of the stakeholders and the public throughout the process.

If the public takes a certain stand, it should be realised that for their proper understanding, besides knowing the extent and targeting the information influence, it is necessary to consider, possibly analyse, objective conditions under which the public takes such stands. Objective conditions include cultural, social, legislative and political situation.

On 25 June 1998, ministers from European countries signed the European Convention on Human Rights in the city of Aarhus, Denmark, which is known as the Aarhus Convention.

The objective of Aarhus Convention was to support the responsibility and transparency of decision-making processes at all levels as well as to strengthen public participation in the environmental and social decision-making. Most of the countries of the United Nations Economic Commission for Europe worked on the preparation of this Convention, and the preparatory process culminated in the signing of this Convention. Adopted document *sets minimum standard for the right to information, public participation in the decision-making process and justice in environmental matters*, which are based on the fact that everyone has the right to a healthy environment in accordance with the sustainable development principles. This does not exclude, however, that the signatories move this standard further. This is what the national governments were invited to do by the representatives of the NGOs during the Aarhus Convention.

There are three pillars to support this kind of decision-making – *the access and right of the public to obtain information on the environment, the right to participate in decisions that affect the environment and the right to justice in environmental matters* (UN ECE, 1998).

In the context of public involvement in the care for landscape environment, *the European Landscape Convention* within the national general measures stipulates an obligation to "create conditions for the participation of general public, local and regional authorities and other parties that are interested in defining and implementing landscape policies aimed at protecting, managing and planning of landscape" (Council of Europe, 2000).

Public participation is about the "public" becoming involved in the whole planning process, actively taking part in the process by which plans and development proposals are created. This involvement can start from the beginning of plan making and can extend to implementation and can involve all aspects of planning, environmental issues, housing, transport and others, and take into account the implications of Aarhus Convention. Many planners have become actively involved in the plan making and implementation process. Modern planning takes the view that the plans belong to the community and community planning should produce plans which are accepted and supported by the community.

In planning theory and practice, politicians and planners are still not aware of the failure of the rational planning model, consisting in a logically structured cycle of decisions. The plea in planning theory for an interactive approach in planning, replacing the rational problem-solving linear approaches, is accompanied by a plea for extensive attention to the representation of the diversity of stakeholders in the policy issues under concern. It is clear that the arguments to pay attention to the representation of all relevant stakeholders, to their possibilities of building up social capital through their representation and active involvement in the interactive and political decision-making processes, are based equally on normative arguments (enhancing equity through the institutionalisation of a more equally spread access to policy making) as they are based on arguments such as increased efficiency of effectiveness.

Appropriate consultation is usually an essential part of planning process. It may take a variety of forms and fulfil many purposes at different process stages. It offers the opportunity to gain advice and help from a wide range of organisations, individuals, local communities and interest groups on a formal and informal basis. It may involve the determining authority, statutory, consultees, amenity and conservation bodies, and local residents.

In the initial stages of landscape management plan/programme, consultation with the planning or other determining authority aims to establish the acceptability of the development objectives.

Statutory consultees may have useful information on landscape and visual assessment. They can provide information on previous landscapes surveys, assessments of the affected area and advice on the basis of landscape and other designations; consultations with these authorities should aim to arrive at consensus on matters such as terms of reference, methodology and assessment techniques.

Consultations with national and local amenity and conservation groups can assist by giving an early indication of key issues that need to be addressed, and by highlighting useful sources of information and expertise. Local schools, local councils and community groups can also assist, for instance, by drawing attention to popular local walks and beauty spots.

A few useful principles for community involvement and public participation include the following:

- Consultation should be genuine and open.
- Avoid to rely exclusively on "consultees list" drawn up for statutory planning consultation procedures.
- The timing of consultation should be carefully planned.
- Requests for participation should be timely.
- Managers should be clear as to the issues on which comment is, and is not, being sought.

The main public consultation methods that can be useful are described in Tab. 3 below.

Community involvement and public participation play an important role in landscape management but require a commitment from managing authorities and consultee to respond positively and constructively. It is a valuable tool in order to reach mutual understanding and agreement on

Tab. 3: Useful consultation methods

• Face-to-face discussion
• Correspondence
• Presentations and informal public meetings
• Exhibitions
• Technical workshops and studio workshops
• Leaflets and mailings
• Photo shooting
• Survey based on an interview questionnaire
• Organising outdoor activities
• Providing access to landscape data via a geoportal

Source: Fischer, 2007

key issues. In addition, it can highlight local interests and values and generate a vision of the ideal landscape after plan or programme development.

Planning and decision-making process in the field of spatial development, in the position of socio-economic, environmental or social, belong to the key implementation issues of democratic governance of development at all hierarchical levels of government, but especially in local politics. As the *integrative function within the complex of spatially relevant planning activities, including protection and landscaping*, is played by the spatial planning, public participation in the land-use planning process has a particular importance.

Participatory approach is a long-term process associated with the development of representative and direct democracy in local government and development of civil society. Decisions on spatial development are often very tense with lots of competing interests. In this difficult interlude of different visions, it is very easy to forget the need to ensure that the community has a sense of *shared ownership of the given land-use* plan. However, it is essential in building long-term commitment to the planned objective. In our country, the local government does not address acute problems of the local community using participatory approach. Some groups, such as investors, land owners and local residents, are involved in discussions on the proposals, but probably do not represent all interests. Other interests may not be directly represented in the debate in the form of pressure groups, commenting entities or supporters. They may include people who receive benefits from the investment (such as prospective employees).

In the early stages of preparation or reviewing the land-use plan, the local government should adopt the role of a mediator between various interests and ensure that those who are not directly represented in the debate can also comment. When the local government has decided which plan to prefer, it may move towards promoting and enshrining role to ensure that the land-use plan is understood and implemented in an environment of subjects of social participation. Such entities include citizens as individuals; municipal authorities; social, cultural and sport organisations; interest groups and citizen initiatives; civic associations and NGOs; entrepreneurs and other economic entities; and expert groups from different areas, which in the pursuit of certain interests in the territory gather in community partnerships.

Decision-makers need active support of the involved public in planning, legislation, implementation and assessment stage of all issues of its territory to:

- provide feedback to specialists in spatial planning;
- understand positions and competences of involved individuals and groups;
- discuss and decide about the direction of the development;
- early identify potential conflict situations so that the conflict can be resolved and to clarify mediation procedures, thereby increasing acceptance;
- strengthen the sense of belonging to the community in resolving local issues;
- develop confidence, communication and understanding;
- increase environmental awareness and disseminate information; and
- provoke broad support for the protection and creation of landscape together with other aspects of the environment.

2
Instruments and tools for sustainable land use and spatial development processes

László Miklós, Anna Špinerová,
Ingrid Belčáková, Andrea Diviaková

2.1 Landscape-Ecological planning (LANDEP)

2.1.1 Background for Landscape-Ecological Planning

Landscape planning in the common sense of the word can be understood as a basic spatial management tool for sustainable landscape development. Several landscape planning instruments in Europe are being applied based on different historical development context, planning and management traditions, background approaches and decision-making processes. They mostly differ in focus and contents. As an important legal support for all of them the European Landscape Convention can be considered that defines landscape planning as "strong forward looking action to enhance, restore or create landscapes" (ELC, 2000). Table 4 illustrates relevant European Landscape Convention definitions.

Tab. 4: Landscape Convention definitions

Box 2. Relevant European Landscape Convention definitions
"Landscape" means an area, as perceived by people, whose character is the result of the action and interaction of natural and/or human factors;
"Landscape policy" means an expression by the competent public authorities of general principles, strategies and guidelines that permit the taking of specific measures aimed at the protection, management and planning of landscapes;
"Landscape quality objective" means, for a specific landscape, the formulation by the competent public authorities of the aspirations of the public with regard to the landscape features of their surroundings;
"Landscape protection" means actions to conserve and maintain the significant or characteristic features of a landscape, justified by its heritage value derived from its natural configuration and/or from human activity;
"Landscape management" means action, from a perspective of sustainable development, to ensure the regular upkeep of a landscape, so as to guide and harmonize changes which are brought about by social, economic and environmental processes;
"Landscape planning" means strong forward-looking action to enhance, restore or create landscapes

Source: Council of Europe, 2000

Landscape planning tools are frequently closely related to optimal and efficient distribution (allocation) of various land use based on landscape-ecological conditions. Such spatial organisation of landscape results in a proposal for most suitable localisation of required human activities within a given territory and, also, in a proposal of necessary measures ensuring the ecologically correct operations of those activities in a given space. But, in others, landscape planning is mainly focused on landscape character and landscape scenery or predominantly on cultural heritage and nature protection.

Several authors remarked that landscape planning instruments/landscape ecology instruments exist in a number of countries (e.g. Austria, France, Germany, Ireland, Italy, the Netherlands, Spain, Sweden and Switzerland) serving as baseline-led instruments that aim at outlining, evaluating and assessing the existing and anticipated status of the landscape, and frequently also of the bio-physical environment for a certain planning area (Herberg, 2000; Joao, 2004; Sheate et al., 2004). In these countries, instruments are designed differently in terms of their objectives, legal status and scope of application. Frequently, anticipated conflicts and impacts connected with future potential land use are also identified. Furthermore, landscape planning normally deals with the establishment of compensation measures for identified impacts of projects, policies, plans and programmes (Schmidt, et al., 2004). The main strength of majority of landscape planning instruments is the capability to provide for some comprehensive environmental baseline data for both planning and management procedures.

2.1.2 LANDEP as the recognised landscape planning methodology

In East European countries, especially in former Czechoslovakia, more attention was given to the landscape ecological point of view based on purposely organised basic research and on its connection with practice. The most complex early conception of applied landscape-ecological methods represented the "potential school" formed in the German Democratic Republic (Haase et al., 1974). Most similar to that complex method was the Landscape-Ecological Planning (LANDEP) programme developed in Slovakia, which the defined "potentials" of complex landscape-ecological units applied as the criteria for the evaluation of their suitability for different human activities (Ružička, Miklós, 1982a).

Landscape-Ecological Planning as a tool of ecologically optimal organisation of the area and thus also a tool for sustainable spatial development is a legally supported part of spatial planning in Slovakia. The methodology of LANDEP was developed at the Institute of Landscape Ecology of the Slovak Academy of Sciences at the turn of the seventies-eighties of the 20th century (Ružička, Miklós, 1979, 1982a, 1982b, 1990). The LANDEP method was recognised and suggested by Agenda 21 (Chapter 10) as a basic methodology for integrated approach to the management of natural resources and landscape as: *"Government on appropriate level should: a) Adopt planning and management systems that facilitate the integration of environmental components such as air, water, land and other natural resources, using landscape ecological planning (LANDEP) or other approaches that focus on, for example, ecosystem or a watershed."* (AGENDA 21, chapter 10, para 1.0.7, page 21. United Nations Conference on Environment and Development, Earth Summit, Rio de Janeiro 1992, July 3rd-12th.)

It is a systemically arranged special complex of applied landscape-ecological methods, the aim of which is to define the suitability of landscape-ecological complexes from the viewpoint of proposed activities and successively the proposal of the ecologically optimum land use (Ružička, Miklós, 1982b).

The landscape-ecological plan has been recognised by the Slovak legislation in the Act of the National Council SR No. 237/2000 in wording of later issued provisions that amends the Act No. 50/1976 on the territorial planning and the construction order (Construction Law). The landscape-ecological plan is defined as the proposal of optimal spatial arrangement and functional exploitation of a territory taking into consideration landscape-ecological, cultural and socio-economic conditions. It is considered to be an integral part of surveys and analyses (§ 19c). The ecologically optimal spatial arrangement and functional use of a territory is defined by this Act as a comprehensive process of mutual harmonisation regarding spatial requests of human economic and other activities facing the landscape-ecological conditions given by the landscape structure of a particular territory. As based on the analysed landscape-ecological conditions, the ecologically optimal spatial arrangement and functional use of the territory proposes the best possible ways of the land use/exploitation of the territory. Thus the application of the landscape-ecological plan into territorial planning documentation answers the:

- requirements to improve and ensure the spatial stabilisation of the territory. The stated criterion is here formed by the demand to achieve the biological balance in the country;
- needs for the protection of nature and natural resources, in particular the protection of the land, water, forests and gene pool;
- needs for the regeneration of human resources and for the protection of human health;
- demands on the humanisation and aesthetisation of the country.

One of the basic output of surveys and analyses is the sketch of main conflicts of interests in a territory (a problem sketch) expressing first of all the limits of land use as ensuing from the generally binding legal provisions, administrative decisions, development plans and intentions and the most serious problems calling for solutions. Precisely, the landscape-ecological plan may play an important role in processing of the quoted conflict-of-interest sketch as the outputs of such plan are:

- map of landscape-ecological complexes, i.e. homogeneous landscape-ecological units of spatial and functional land use;
- map of environmental problems, i.e. specification and identification of environmental problems that result of stress factor effects on nature, on natural resources and the environment;
- map of alternative ecological selection. A set of feasible activities is defined for each area. It means the selection of activities, which are not limited by any feature of landscape-forming components;
- map of ecologically optimal land use. It represents the ideal activities for a given area including the ecostabilising measures.

Thus the landscape-ecological plan presents the main binding landscape-ecological regulation of the legally recognised territorial-planning documentation.

2.1.3 The frame of the methodical procedure of the LANDEP

From the theoretical-methodological point of view, LANDEP represents an applied landscape-ecological approach to the ecologisation of the spatial organisation of landscape.

The ecologisation of the spatial organisation of the landscape is a process aimed at a proposal for the ecologically most suitable *localisation* of required human activities within a given territory and successively in a proposal of *necessary measures* ensuring the ecologically correct operation of those activities in a given locality. Thus it is a methodology to answer the questions of *where* and *how* to place human activities in the territory that they are in the least contradiction with the natural conditions (Ružička, Miklós, 1982b, 1990, Miklós, 1992; Miklós, Špinerová, 2011).

The central conception of the process of ecologisation rests upon the understanding of landscape as a geosystem, as the complex of the elements and their relation, as defined scientifically, as well as in the Act of the National Council SR No. 237/2000 §139a (3) *"Landscape is a complex system of space, location, georelief and other mutually, functionally inter-*

connected material natural elements and elements modified and created by a man, in particular geological basement and soil creating substratum, water bodies, soil, flora and fauna, artificial objects and elements of utilisation of territory, as well as their connection determined by socio-economic phenomena in the society. Landscape is the environment of the man and other living organisms."

2.1.4 LANDEP methodology

The basic methodology of LANDEP is relatively broadly conceived and contains a relatively complicated method (Miklós, 1979). Therefore, this method should be simplified (e.g. the so-called ecological evaluation of the territory that has been worked out for the needs of territorial planning).

The LANDEP method is based on a thorough landscape-ecological analysis and successive synthesis. Types of landscape-ecological complexes bear the indices of ecological properties of the landscape - suppositions for performing social activities. The core of applied part of the LANDEP - the evaluations and propositions - is based on the confrontation and successive proposal of the way of harmonisation as to

- the complex of the *properties* of types of landscape-ecological complexes on the one side, and
- the demands and influences of human activities on those properties on the other side.

Data obtained are interpreted into a form usable in the process of landscape-ecological evaluation. In the process of evaluation, the social activities are compared with landscape properties in order to answer three essential questions (Ružička, Miklós, 1982b, Miklós, 1992):

- How is a given set of ecological properties of the landscape adapted to functional claims of social activities, i.e. to what extent can some activity be developed in a given area?
- What effects have incidental localisation of some activity had on the properties of a given area?
- What is the present state of natural and anthropically conditioned processes and properties of the landscape (stability, balance, resistance, etc.)?

Formally, the methodological procedure of LANDEP consists of the following steps (Ružička, Miklós, 1982, see Fig. 1):

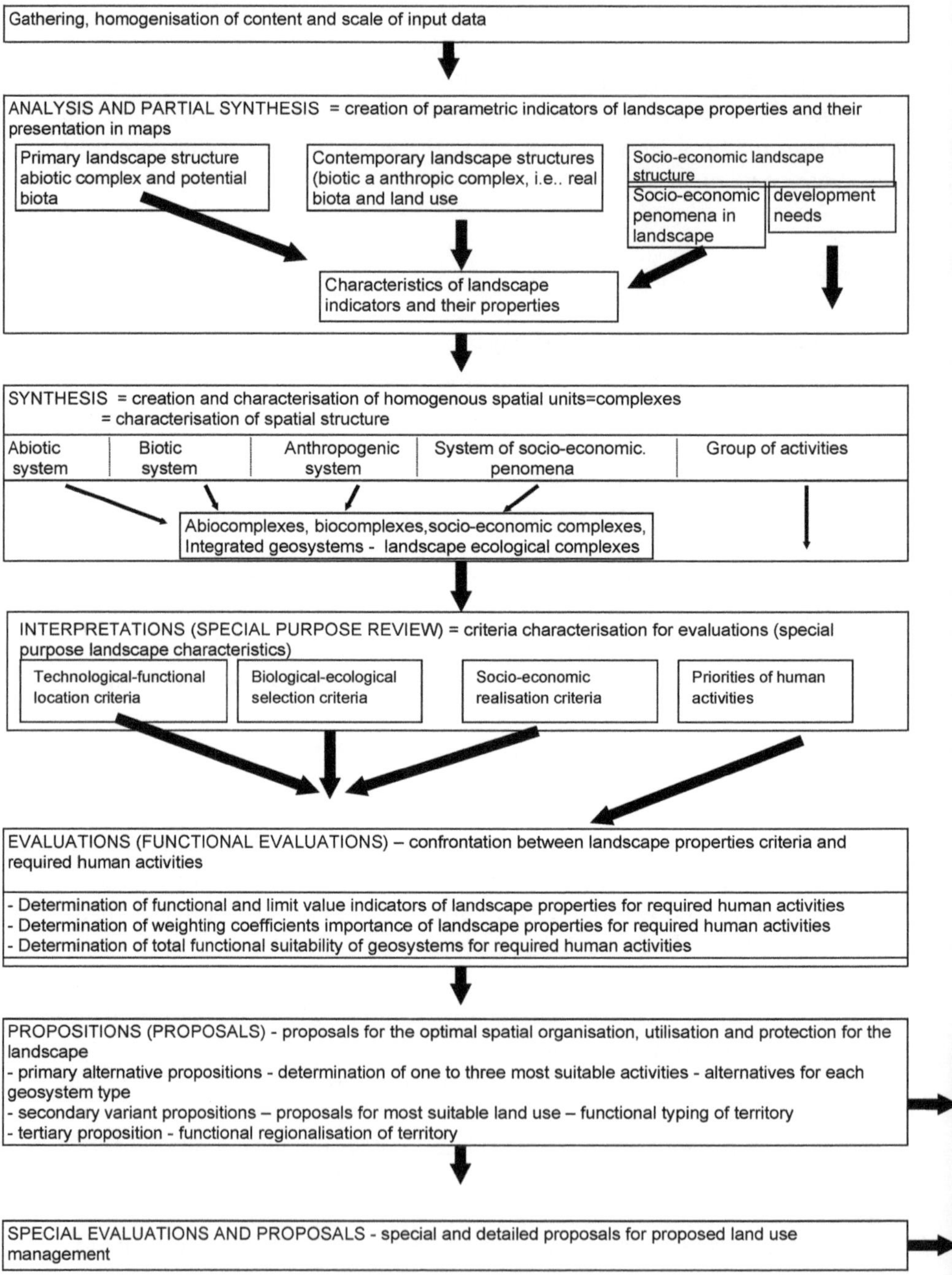

Fig. 1: LANDEP Scheme (Miklós, Špinerová, 2011)

I. Analyses

The principal objective of analyses is to select, quantify and describe the main properties of abiotic, biotic and socio-economic complexes determining the ecologisation of the spatial organisation of landscape. The most important analyses are:

- analyses of geomorphologic, geological, hydrological, soil and climatic conditions (properties of the abiotic complex of the territory);
- analyses of fauna and flora and their conditions (properties of the biotic complex of the territory);
- analyses of socio-economic activities and their negative influences (properties of the socio-economic complex of the territory).

The result is then the elaboration of a set of cartographic representations concerning the characteristics of the properties of abiotic, biotic and socio-economic elements in the given territory.

II. Syntheses

The syntheses are based on a superposition of selected indicators regarding the properties of abiotic, biotic and socio-economic complexes in the territory. The aim of the syntheses is to create and characterise the homogeneous areas with various combinations of abiotic, biotic and socio-economic indicators of the region, e.g. the so-called the integral geosystems. This step results in synthetic units, i.e. types of the landscape ecological complex consisting of abiocomplexes (see Fig. 2): the present landscape structure, complexes of the positive socio-economic phenomena, complexes of the negative socio-economic phenomena, and complexes of natural stress factors. The types have their real spatial expression on maps with different combinations of natural and socio-economical landscape indicators.

III. Interpretations

The interpretations express the creation of criteria for the evaluation. In practical form they show the character of functional landscape properties/indices. It is possible to divide functional landscape indices into four fundamental groups (Miklós, 1995; Miklós, Špinerová, 2011):

- localisational (technological-abiotic) indices – physical conditions for the realisation of different activities;
- selective (ecological-biotic) indices – aspects of the maintenance of eco-

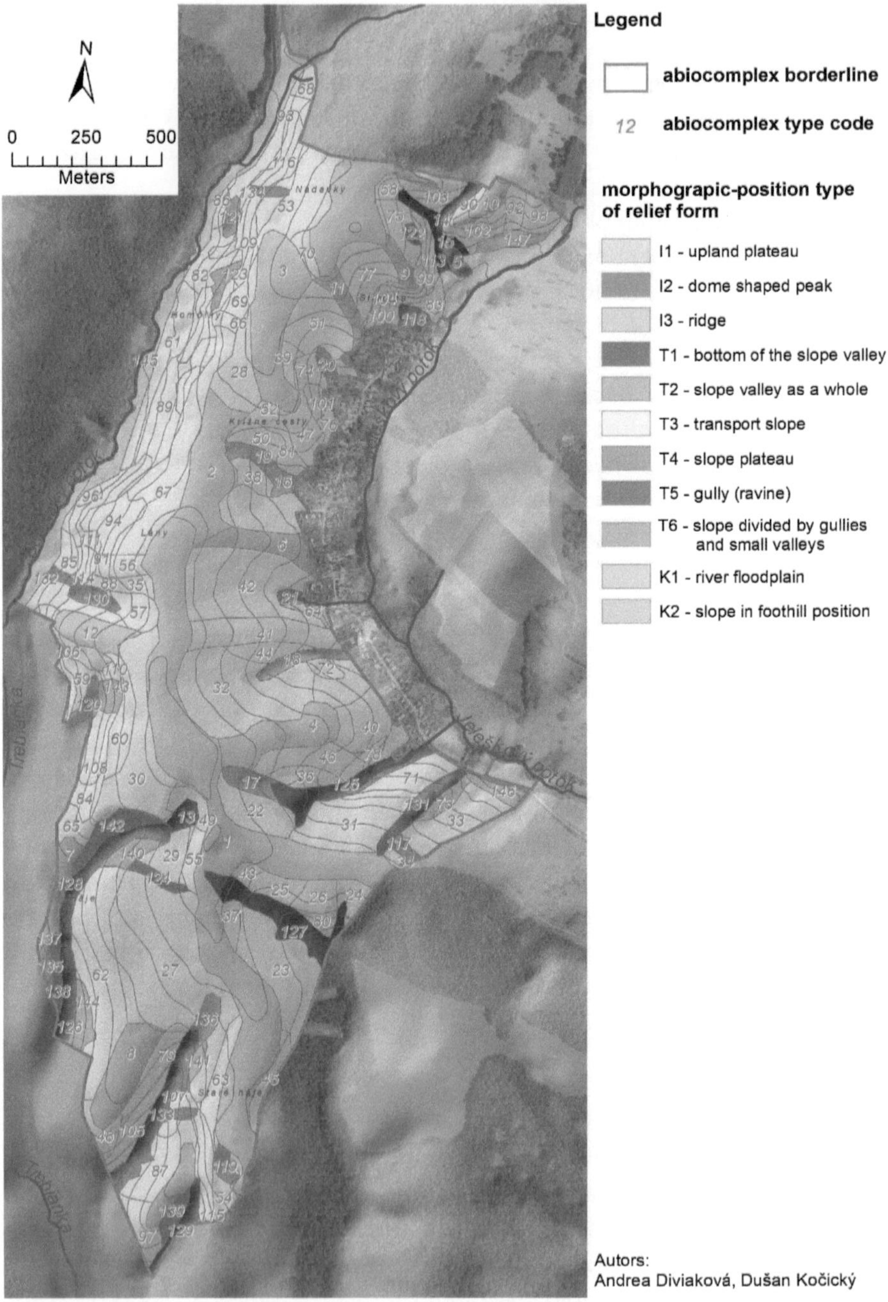

Fig. 2: Abiocomplexes (Diviaková, Kočický, 2012)

logical stability and biodiversity of landscape, aspects of the maintenance of nature and natural resources;
- realisational (socio-economical) indices - aspects of the active influence of human activities and actual stage of the environment, aspects of environmental care;
- indices of human requirements and their categories of priority - as intensive demands of the society on the use of the territory as possible.

IV. Evaluations

This step represents a confrontation between the values of landscape indexes and the requirements of human activities. The process of evaluation consists of the following steps:
- determination of the functional suitability values (especially ecologically limited and determined values) of individual indexes for each human activity;
- determination of the weighted coefficients of individual indexes for each human activity;
- determination of the total suitability value of each geosystem for each human activity.

Determination of the suitability of landscape properties for the location of selected social activities is carried out via identification of factors limiting the performance of individual socio-economic activities. Few of the basic aspects for such evaluation can be listed as follows (Hrnčiarová, Izakovičová, 2000; Miklós, Špinerová, 2011):
- abiotic conditions regarding the permanent unchangeable character of their elements should be considered the determining factors for different forms of land use, thus also for other aspects of the socio-economic development;
- in localities susceptible and prone to manifestations of degradation processes (localities prone to erosion-accumulation processes, landslides, earthquakes and the like) in the consequence of socio-economic activities, a form of land use palliating the negative manifestation of the quoted factors should be carried out;
- in protected territories, ecologically valuable and stable territories (localities of the territorial system of ecological stability), it is necessary to prioritise the development of activities that do not threaten natural assets of the landscape, such as research and science, nature conservation or therapeutic and recreation activities.

- likewise, it is necessary to exclude development of such socio-economic activities that could possibly affect individual natural resources in the territories with legally stipulated protection of natural resources and to prefer development of activities connected with the support to protective functions of natural resources;
- activities sensitive to hygienic parameters of the environment are excluded from areas with a severe load of stress factors such as air pollution, soil and water pollution or noise overload;
- territories free from the load of stressfactors are not suitable for location of different industries/businesses that might threaten the current satisfactory hygienic quality. They are suitable first of all for the activities demanding high quality hygienic parameters such as housing, recreation, amenities, growing of crops for direct consumption, wine growing, etc.

Pragmatically, one of the main aims of the evaluations is the assessment of the suitability of the present functional use of the territory and to define those ecologically problematic areas in which the present land use does not correspond with ecological criteria. In other words, to identify the areas where the present land use is restricted by some of the ecological factors. Consecutively, the aim of the newly proposed, ecologically optimum use of the territory is to eliminate these problem areas, to foresee possible new problems and thus to create a spatial structure which is in harmony with the natural and socio-economic conditions of the territory.

V. Propositions

This point represents the final phase of the methodical procedure. Its goal is to propose a landscape-ecologically-optimum way of the spatial organisation and utilisation of landscape. It has two aspects:

a) aspect of spatial organisation expressing an optimum land use;
b) technological aspect expressing the ecologisation of technology used in the landscape.

A proposal of landscape-ecologically optimal land use consists of:

- setting an alternative ecological choice. A set of activities feasible in a given area which are not limited by any of landscape-forming components is defined;
- setting of an ecologically optimal way of land use – selection of the optimal socio-economic activity for a given area;
- definition of landscape-ecological measures pursuing the typology of specified landscape ecological problems, namely:

- measures focused on the improvement of the territorial ecological stability and biodiversity;
- measures protecting natural and cultural/historical resources;
- measures aimed at the improvement of environmental quality; and aesthetics.

The basic method of LANDEP expressed in Fig. 1 is arranged so that it may be modified or simplified. However, a logical framework is preserved in every modified method so that the three above-mentioned essential questions are solved.

2.1.5 Implementation of landscape-ecological regulations into territorial-planning documentations in Slovakia

The result of the decision-making process of ecologisation of the spatial organisation and functional utilisation of the territory in technical sense is the determination of the limiting indicators (limits and restrictions) for the localisation and realisation of individual activities resulting from landscape-ecological plan and/or from the projects of the territorial system of ecological stability. Determining the limiting values requires an extensive process through the LANDEP from the collection of data up to the propositions because the successful implementation of every human activity is to a certain degree dependent upon a wide variety of factors of the territory in which the activities are carried out. Therefore the properties of landscape as a whole as well as those of its individual components represent certain limits for the localisation and realisation of individual activities.

The Act of the National Council SR No. 237/2000 defines the regulations as the values of the properties of the components of the landscape structure, as reads the §139a (1)*"Regulation of spatial arrangement and functional utilisation of territory is a binding guideline which guides the localisation and arrangement of a certain object or realisation of a certain activity in territory. It is expressed through values of properties of components of landscape structure by words, figures and graphically, if possible. Regulation has a character of bans, limitations or supporting factors in relation to spatial arrangement and functional utilisation of territory. In this way regulator determines banned, limited and acceptable activity or function in territory."*

The determined indicators as ecological limits may exclude the realisation of a social activity in a given area. This concerns the determination of indicators that – from the viewpoint of ecological principles – do not allow the use of a certain area for a given activity. For example, one of the limits for the development of industry is the size of protected areas. We understand the determined values and indicators that significantly limit the intensity of a given activity in an area, although they do not absolutely exclude it, as restrictions. For example, in an area protected because of water, the agricultural production is not excluded but its intensity is considerably restricted by the recommended structure of crops, by the restricted use of chemicals and mechanisation, etc. (Izakovičová, 2000).

The determination of ecological limits and restrictions allows an objective and scientific decision-making on the localisation of social activities in the landscape. It is necessary to add that this is a very complicated and time-consuming process demanding a multi-disciplinary and synergistic approach. It starts from the existing norms in the society and conditions in nature. If there is no stated norm for a given phenomenon or social activity, the approach starts from a collective evaluation of experts. In general, a set of regulations, limits and restrictions includes the following categories (Izakovičová 2000):

a) regulations of abiotic components: Their values are conditioned by the characteristics of the abiotic complex. Geomechanical, hydrological, aerodynamic and pedological limits and restrictions belong here. These factors are of a permanent character and can not be easily changed by technology (e.g. the relative stability of the geological substratum, climate).
b) regulations of biotic components: Their values are derived from the characteristics of the biotic complex. They arise from the needs of living organisms. Up to now, the biotic limits and restrictions have been respected very little in practice. This situation threatens both gene pool and the ecological stability of the country.
c) regulations of anthropic components: They result from the demands and requirements of socio-economic activities that – through their negative effects or by simple using an area – limit and restrict the development of other activities. They comprise, e.g. technical, hygienic, protective and other limits and restrictions. Compared to the preceding types of limits, these indicators can be changed relatively easier, e.g. by the termination of production or by the installation of a filter plant. Although the anthropogenic regulations have the character of temporary limits and restrictions, they represent the group of very serious hygienic limits and restrictions.

2.2 Territorial System of Ecological Stability (TSES) and spatial planning practice

2.2.1 Ecological stability of the ecosystem and spatial ecological stability of the landscape

The starting point and basic criterion for assessing the spatial stability of the landscape is the internal *environmental quality - stability of ecosystems*. Ecological stability is defined differently by different authors; one acceptable definition is "the ability of ecosystems to persist during operational disturbance, to store and reproduce their essential characteristics under conditions of interference from the outside" (Míchal, 1992). This ability expresses *resistance*, i.e. minimal changes during the operation of disturbance or resilience (the ability to return to the baseline).

Buček and Lacina (1995) distinguish internal and external ecological stability:

- *Internal (endogenous) ecological stability* is the ability of the ecosystem to exist under normal exposure to environmental factors, those that the ecosystem is adapted to. It is determined by the strength and the amount of internal links in the ecosystem. High internal ecological stability is characteristic of climax communities (natural and indigenous).
- *External (exogenous) ecological stability* is the ability of the ecosystem to resist external factors that the ecosystem is not adapted to through natural development (temperature fluctuations, fires, earthquakes, volcanic eruptions, air pollution, changes in the hydrological regime, of chemicalisation of agricultural production and so on).
- Spatial ecological stability of the landscape is therefore a dynamic measure of the ability to maintain the present landscape structure of both vertical and horizontal ecological relations in the landscape at an acceptable conventional (model) level even if the landscape is formed in particulars by various ecosystems with low levels of ecological stability.

Preserving the spatial ecological stability of the landscape is *the meaning of creating ecological networks.*

2.2.2 Spatial configuration and composition of the landscape

Spatial ecological structure of the landscape is often considered the core issue of landscape ecology. Many authors have conducted research into spatial relations of ecosystems, spatial arrangement, and spatial impact of ecosystems on their surroundings. This research attempts to demonstrate the significance of ecologically stable landscape elements due to their spatial influence. Spatially interconnected, ecologically stable landscape elements are generally referred to as *ecological networks*. Methodologies for this focus are flourishing throughout the world and also include the methodology of TSES.

The theoretic basis for forming views addressing the issue of habitat fragmentation and concept of ecological networks is island biogeography (Mac Arthur, Wilson, 1967), which was later developed as metapopulation theory, which was the focus of Opdam et al. (1995) and Hanski (1998).

Forest fragments in farmland or isolated wetlands may be considered pseudo-islands, but they are governed by similar rules as true islands. Here too the direct correlation between the size of a natural element, its shape or even distance from the nearest similar habitat and species diversity can be observed. The surrounding landscape also plays an important role as it is prone to change induced by anthropogenic activities. The theory of island biogeography managed to quantify these relations. One of the major factors affecting species diversity of true and pseudo-islands is the size of the habitat fragment (direct correlation) and the degree of isolation (inverse correlation). Ecological networks are designed to preserve the minimum area required for survival of natural communities or target vulnerable populations, and mitigate the isolation effects resulting from the isolation of landscape elements in the anthropogenic landscape, e.g. by means of designating biocorridors, and, in extreme cases, by technical solutions, such as ecoducts.

Metapopulation theory deals with the behaviour of the populations in the landscape with fragmented habitats inhabited also by smaller subpopulations. It treats basic demographic trends (natality, mortality, migrality, etc.) as indicative monitoring characteristics of each population. Furthermore, it emphasises the importance of communication between subpopulations and considers a possibility of replacing locally extinct subpopulations. The findings and results of metapopulation theory also address necessity of preserving or restoring interconnectivity of landscape elements in the anthropogenic landscape.

Fragmentation of habitats affects various types of organisms differently. The metapopulation theory explains the impact of fragmentation on different populations. Increasing anthropogenic pressure in fragmented agricultural landscapes results in reduced size and quality of patches and increased resistance (eliminating of hedgerows), which consequently upsets the balance between the rate of extinction and recolonisation, to the extent where, on average, fewer patches are colonised. As the proportion of empty patches grows, the probability of species subsistence decreases. Current trends and research confirms the relevance of the theoretical basis for the concept of ecological networks in the landscape.

A coherent spatial structure builds on the approach of Forman, Godron (1986, 1993), who promoted the evolutionary theory of patches and the landscape matrix, which can be subsequently employed in planning, and designing of corridors.

Corridors and patches are important and ubiquitous landscape features. Their origin and character is affected by disruption, heterogeneity of landscape resources and anthropic impacts. The final result of the process is exceptionally diverse species dynamics, stability and change. The key aspect of corridors is their interconnectivity or the presence of gaps. The patch-corridor-matrix paradigm introduced by Forman, Godron (1986, 1993) enhanced the understanding and analysis of the landscape as a whole in terms of the developmental dynamics of its individual components. The theory allows the analysis of landscape elements as well as the relations existing between them.

2.2.3 Ecological networks and the Territorial System of Ecological Stability (TSES)

Establishing of ecological networks is currently one of the main objectives of landscape ecology and nature and landscape protection. It is based on important international documents such as Agenda 21, the UN Convention on Biological Diversity, the Pan-European Biological and Landscape Diversity Strategy, EECONET under the European program of IUCN, the European Landscape Convention. After all, the principles of NATURA 2000 also articulate the need to preserve the network of significant ecosystems. International policies and programmes constitute a foundation for developing national programmes of ecological networks.

However, ecological networks have several different interpretations. The scientific basis for creating ecological networks is exceptionally complex and requires clarification of the functioning of the ecological stability of landscape and its significance for nature as well as man. The set of protected areas which is often characterised as an ecological network can basically be classified into three groups:

a) The network of protected areas of *"natural heritage"* significance. This is a set of traditionally protected areas, typically the most natural and best-preserved areas, rare habitats, curiosities, national peculiarities and endemic phenomena. It is a *cultural-natural-historical approach to ecological networks of the character of the* natural heritage. Such areas form a significant experimental basis for ecological research. They are not, in the strict sense, ecological networks; they are not interconnected and the spatial relationships of these areas are irrelevant. Such a network is built from the oldest national conservation areas, which include the *network of European Diploma Sites (1965) and the European network of biosphere reserves* MAB ("Man and Biosphere") dating from 1976. These are the initial activities of the UNESCO in the field of ecological networks.

Sites network covers the list of nature reserves of European importance and serves as a prime example of natural heritage. The European diploma was awarded based on the following criteria: (1) representativeness, (2) historic, aesthetic, scientific or recreational value determined by the particular characteristics of fauna, flora, geology, climate and geographical situation and (3) protection status (Jongman, 1995). The European diplomas are awarded for 5 years, and after this period the reserve is evaluated for threats, quality and management and if the criteria are not met, the diploma is revoked.

b) The network of various protected *"landscape types"*. It is a *physical-(bio) geographical* approach to the establishment of ecological networks. The aim is to preserve as many representative landscape types as possible. The focus is mostly on natural or endangered landscape types. This method is the most commonly employed and widespread worldwide. It is not built on real spatially interconnected systems. This group includes the NATURA 2000 system.

c) Spatial ecological systems in the real sense of the word are spatial networks aimed at preserving both the internal functions and spatial relationships in the whole range of ecosystems (not only the natural ones), i.e. the emphasis is put on *maintaining spatial relations* and not the quality of selected ecosystems or territories. It is a *landscape-ecological approach* to creation of ecological networks. This approach forms the basis for modern concepts of *territorial systems of ecological stability*.

TSES is a type of ecological network based on the original principles produced by the landscape-ecological school in Brno and Bratislava, at that time as a part of the comprehensive rationalising brigade (Buček, Lacina, 1984; Buček, Lacina, Löw, 1984; Jurko, 1986; Miklós, 1986; Miklós, Kozová, Ružička, et al., 1986) and other workplaces. The concept of TSES was incorporated in the policy of environmental protection following legislative changes instigated by the Slovak Commission for the Environment immediately after its founding (Miklós 1991).

TSES represents the most significant integration of landscape ecology principles into real environment policies and spatial planning practice. It has become a part of the legislation, general ecological regulation of various plans and projects and it has become a common part of decision-making processes, *as well as land-use planning procedures at all hierarchical levels.*

2.2.4 Principles of the methodology of Territorial System of Ecological Stability

Methodology of the LANDEP (**Land**scape-**E**cological **P**lanning) creates the theoretical and methodical frame for projecting of the territorial system of ecological stability.

In Slovakia, the TSES serves as an obligatory part of all territorial planning documentation. It represents the whole-scale structure of mutually linked ecosystems, their parts and elements; it ensures the sustainability of life forms and life conditions in the landscape and, at the same time, it creates the conditions for the sustainable development of landscape. Ecological optimisation of spatial organisation of the landscape presented by the LANDEP methodology is a systemically organised complex of landscape ecological methodologies and techniques (Ružička Miklós, 1982b), and thus the methodological procedures employed by LANDEP constitute a basis for elaboration of the TSES documents (MŽP SR, 1993; Izakovičová et al., 2000).

After gradual development of its methodology, the TSES can be defined as follows:

The Territorial System of Ecological Stability (TSES) is a whole-territory system of an ecologically optimum structure of a landscape composed of individual elements with different degrees of ecological stability and different uses, but in its entirety ensuring

- *internal functioning of individual core ecosystems;*
- *functionality of the spatial relations* among them as a precondition for the maintenance of the spatial landscape-ecological stability and so diversity of both conditions and forms of life.

TSES has two equally important essential parts:

- *the skeleton of TSES* (a system of biocentres and biocorridors);

- *a system of ecostabilising measures* Miklós, 1996; Miklós, Diviaková, Izakovičová, 2011).

Both these parts are of the same importance and functioning of TSES can be maintained only by safeguarding both of them.

Based on the theoretical and methodological principles, numerous practical procedures of preparation of TSES projects have been elaborated. As the practical procedures are expected to improve over time, we will identify only the principles that enable further elaboration of practical methodologies in the future.

The elements of TSES are the most varied geoecosystems. To maintain the desired state of the system, it is crucial to sustain adequate ecological relations between them. The key elements of the skeleton of TSES – biocentres, biocorridors and interactive elements need to ensure proper functioning of the following critical relationships (Miklós, 1995, Law no. 543/2002):

a) *Biocentres* maintain the food chain as well as the conditions for a reproductive cycle (reproduction and raising offspring) and provide protection, resting place and shelter. These are the cornerstone of the TSES and should be formed with ecologically most stable elements of the landscape structure (forest, greenery, grasslands, wetlands, natural water areas, etc.).
b) *Biocorridors and interactive* elements facilitate overcoming barriers that isolate ecosystems and maintain the exchange of genetic information and migration as well as the interaction between various ecosystems with different degrees of ecological stability (particularly important are linear communities and ecotones). From spatial and functional standpoint they are represented by the elements of landscape structure providing the interconnection between the biocentres. Emphasis is given here above all on the position of the element in the framework of the whole spatial structure of the country.
c) *Buffer zones and interactive element* is a specific ecosystem or a group of ecosystems and its elements (e.g. permanent grassland, swamp, forest, lake) that are interconnected with biocentres and biocorridors, which positively affect the surrounding parts of the landscape changed or disturbed by human activities.

Ecosystems with a high degree of ecological stability (forests, landscape greenery, grasslands) perform at the same time also different practical ecological functions – ecostabilising functions – such as soil and water protection, microclimatic, hygienic, aesthetic and others.

In reality, however, biocorridors for numerous species (especially the more mobile ones) are often spatially disconnected. For example, in our conditions, the biocorridors of xerothermic species may consist of a chain of more or less spatially unlinked (isolated) lower-level biocentres at the regional and higher level. The same view has been expressed by the authors of the European ecological network EECONET (Bennet, 1991).

The *system of measures* leading to an ecologically optimum organisation and utilisation of landscape is also an inevitable part of TSES.

2.2.5 The methodology of the Territorial System of Ecological Stability (TSES)

The methodological procedure of TSES has consisted of five main steps: analyses, syntheses, classification, evaluation, and proposals. A schema of dependency of main elements of TSES methodology is in Fig. 3.

2.2.5.1 Analyses and Syntheses

A principal objective of the analyses is to choose, quantify and describe the main properties of a biotic, an abiotic and a socio-economical complex, which determine the creation of TSES.

The basis of the TSES analyses is to draw a map of the present landscape structure (PLS) characterising the present state of land utilisation of the territory. This makes it possible to define the really existing natural ecosystems of the territory.

Analyses of abiotic factors are especially unavoidable to quantify factors influencing a variety of life conditions in a given territory. Analyses of geomorphologic, furthermore, geological, hydrological, soil and climatic conditions create the basis of analyses of abiotic complex of territory (see Fig. 4-6).

The central feature of the biotic factors analyses is in evaluation of significant gene pool localities of fauna and flora. These analyses also included an assessment of potential geosystems representing a diversity of particular territorial ecosystems. This step needs to be performed in order to localise some additional elements of the TSES.

The analysis of socio-economic conditions includes two basic groups as follows:

a) the analysis of the socio-economic activities oriented to a conservation of nature and the natural resources – this leads to a spatial definition of landscape areas preserved by legislation (such as protected territories,

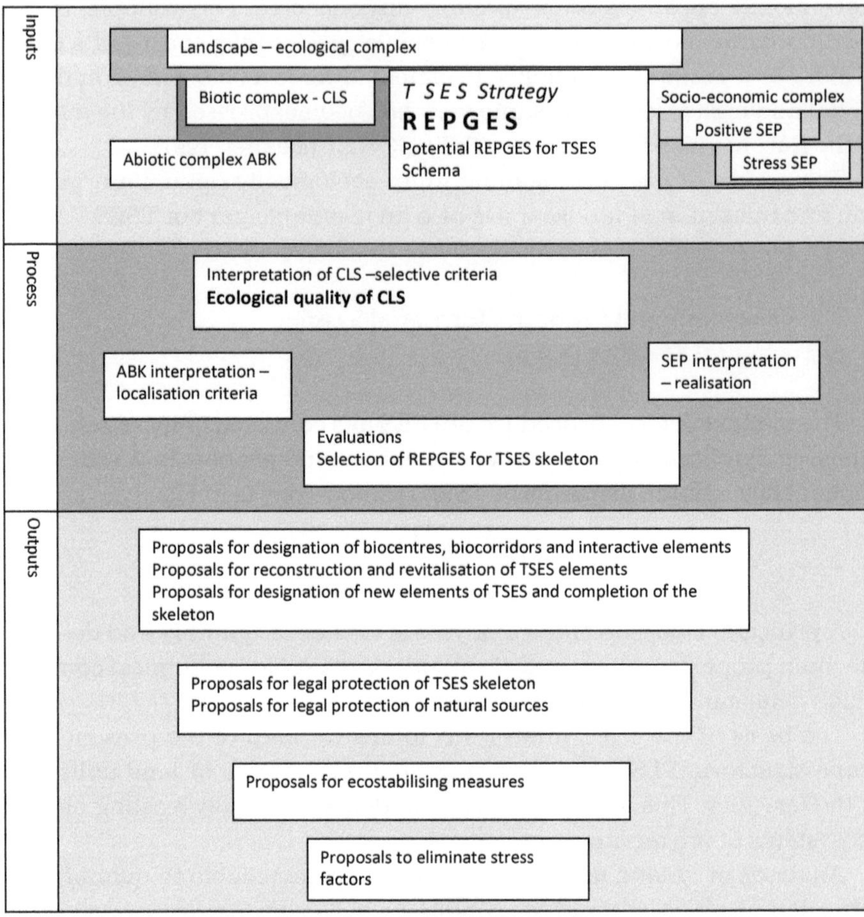

Fig. 3: Schema of approach for creating TSES project (Miklós, Diviaková, Izakovičová, 2011)

hygienically protected zones of water sources, purpose-utilised forests, protected soils, etc.);

b) the analysis of the socio-economic phenomena corresponding to stress factors that threaten basic elements of the TSES.

The syntheses are based on a superposition of selected analytical indicators. As an important result of the syntheses, two synthetic maps may be considered:

c) a map of the positive elements of the territory – represents the spatial differentiation of ecologically valuable segments of the land such as gene pool localities, protected territories, and others;

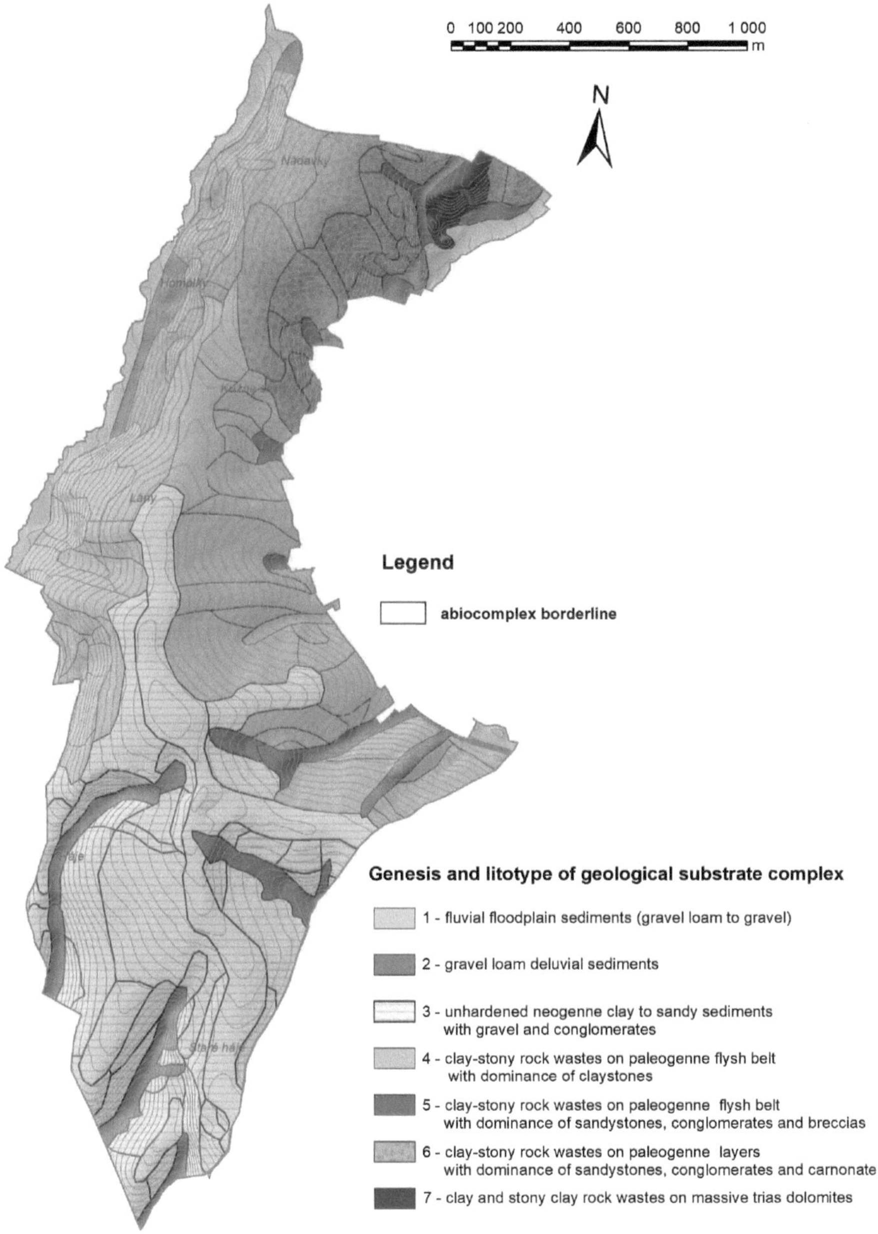

Fig. 4: Genésis and litotype (Kočický, 2012 in Diviaková, Kočický, Novikmec, Svitok, 2012)

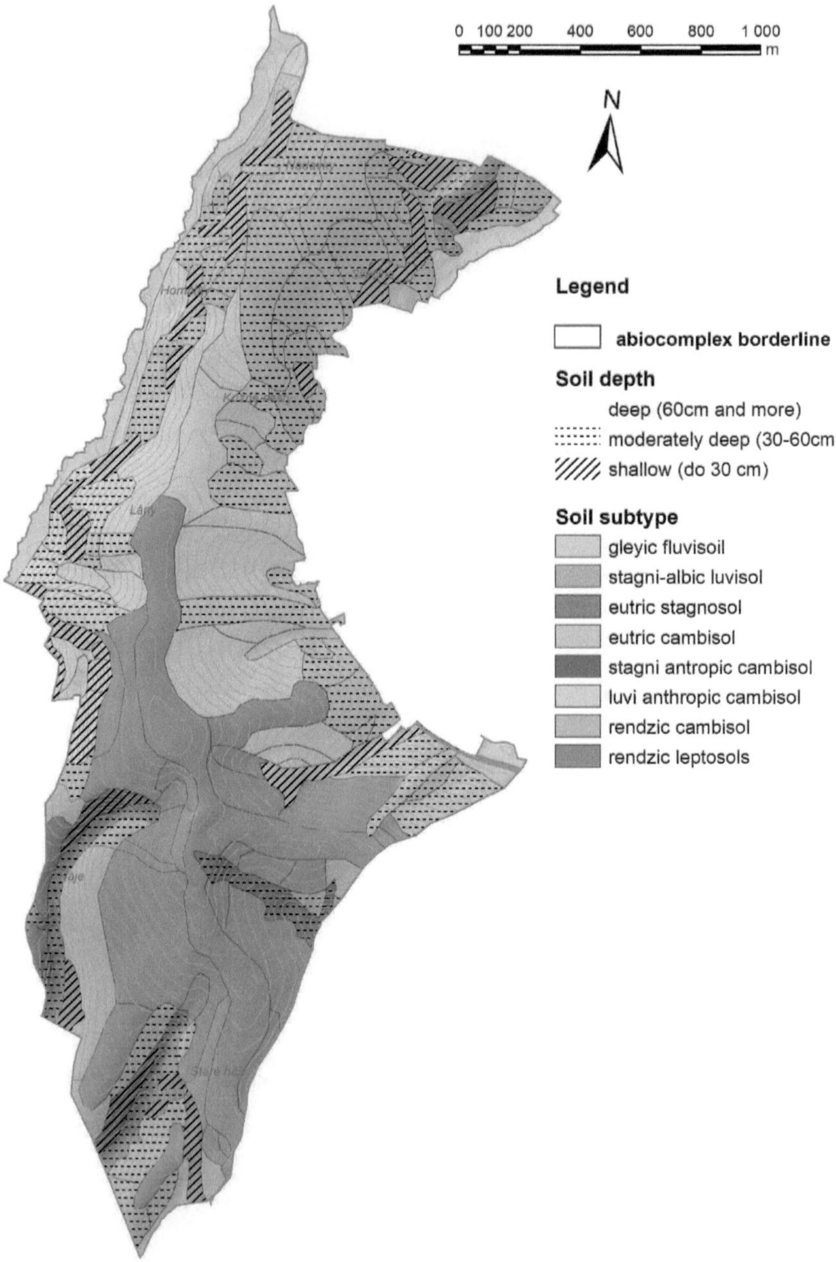

Fig. 5: Soil subtypes (Kočický, 2012 in Diviaková, Kočický, Novikmec, Svitok, 2012)

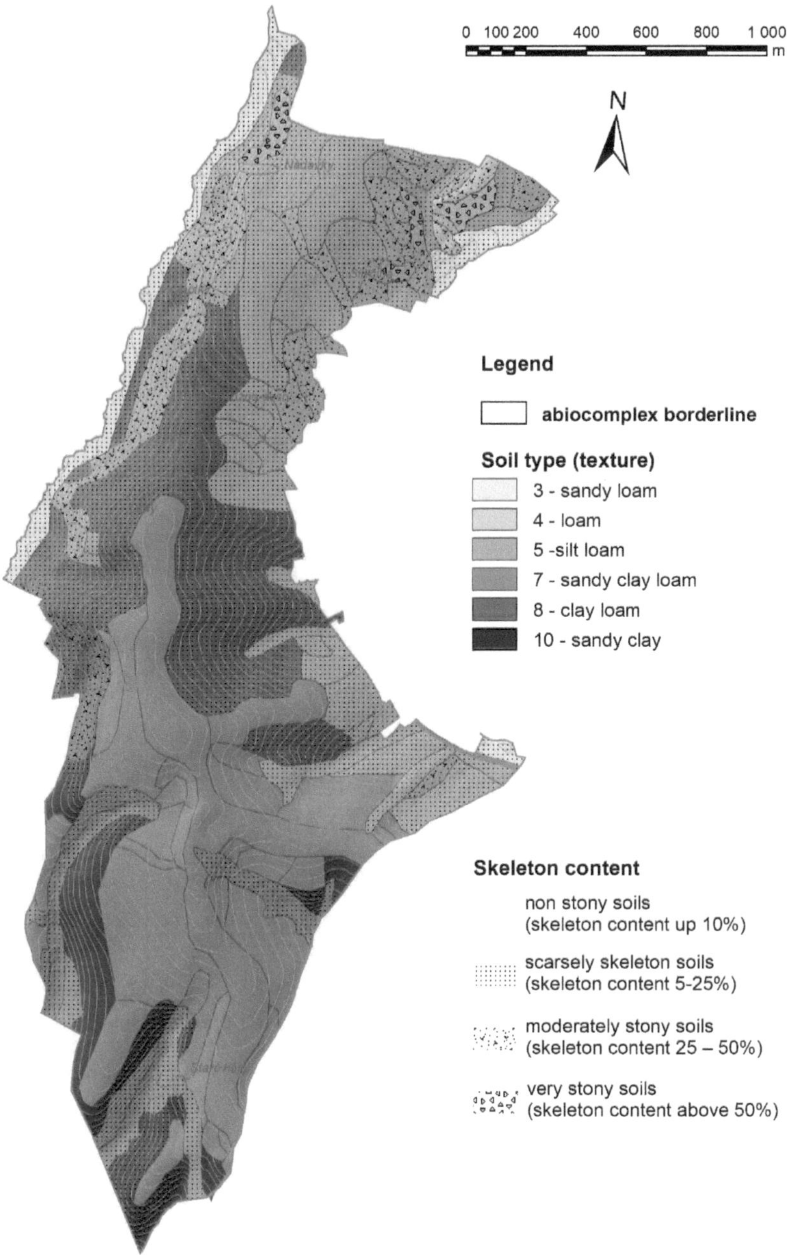

Fig. 6: Soil types (Kočický, 2012 in Diviaková, Kočický, Novikmec, Svitok, 2012)

d) a map of negative elements of the territory – represents a spatial synthesis of factors threatening the biodiversity of the territory.

2.2.5.2 Classification and evaluation

The result is the classification of territory starting from evaluation of the ecological state. The main criteria for classification are as follows:

e) factors supporting ecological stability;
f) factors reducing ecological stability.

This step is aimed at the specification of environmental problems resulting from territorial conflicts of two territorial systems – territorial system of ecological stability and territorial system of stress factors. The result of this step is

- identification of localities threatened with natural stress factors – erosion, waterlogging, drought;
- identification of localities threatened with anthropogenic stress factors – emission, noise, odour, dust;
- identification of conflicts between ecologically important segments and stress factors – identification of environmental problems.

Proposition

It is the final step of the TSES projecting aimed at the characteristics of a desired, ecologically optimum structure of the territory as well as at the characteristics of necessary measures for the maintenance of such structure. However, it is a complex procedure realised according to the following steps:

1. *proposals of the TSES framework: the network of biocentres and biocorridors* – they are based mostly on the analyses of the present landscape structure and legal conditions. This group of proposals consists of the following categories:
   - proposal and characterisation of the network of biocentres;
   - proposal and characterisation of the network of biocorridors;
   - proposal for location of new elements of TSES;
   - reconstruction of biocentres and biocorridors.
2. *proposal for protection* with the aim of protecting the existing and proposed elements of the TSES. Proposals for protection consist of the following groups:

- the confirmation of the existing status (existing protected areas);
- proposals to strengthen the existing status (in order to enhance the protection level);
- proposals to declare the TSES elements protected.

3. *proposals of eco-stabilising measures* aimed at the stabilisation of the landscape system, protection of nature and natural resources. The proposals of eco-stabilising measures consist of the following:
   - proposals for the localisation of new eco-stabilizing elements with the aim of stabilising the agricultural landscape by placing the groups and zones of non-forest tree and shrubby vegetation etc.;
   - proposals for the ecologically optimum use of the agricultural landscape with the aim of changing cultivation and the crop structure as well as taking agrotechnical and special agroecological measures derived from the properties of abiotic complexes in the territory;
   - proposals of eco-stabilising measures in the forest ecosystems directed towards ensuring the renewal of the natural composition of forest ecosystems in the territory, preventing the monoculturisation of forest ecosystems, etc.;
   - proposals to eliminate stress factors in the landscape, consisting of technological measures, measures to remove the results of contamination and finally measures to limit the effects resulting from transport operations, etc.

Preparing the TSES results in a system of proposals which we can divide into the following:

a) *proposals for the elements of the TSES skeleton – biocentres and biocorridors.* An important component of these proposals is the proposal to maintain or strengthen the current legislative protection of existing features as well as proposals to create new elements, if a particular region does not appear to have the necessary representative ecosystems, as an appropriate biocentre or biocorridor.
b) *proposals to improve the overall ecological quality of the present landscape structure.* This step consists primarily in a proposal for land-use changes, especially the structure and location of non-forest tree and shrub vegetation and grasslands. These can be seen as a part of biocorridors and interactive elements.
c) *proposals of ecostabilising measures.* These are secured by the overall functioning of TSES. They are particularly proposals for optimal use of land, proposals for agrotechnical, agrochemical and agro-amelioration measures.

d) *proposals for necessary legislative measures* to ensure proper functionality of selected TSES elements.

TSES can be considered complete only if it incorporates the proposals contained in all the aforementioned groups. It is a comprehensive and whole-space TSES.

Proposals for legal protection of elements of TSES can have the following forms:

a) *including protected areas* in the TSES site and determining their functions – this is confirmation of the current state of protection of the individual elements of TSES with positive socio-economic phenomenas (SEP). For the given element of TSES, the level of protection is defined (from 2nd to 5th degree).
b) *proposal for strengthening current protection* – a proposal for the re-classification of the degree of protection of TSES elements, mostly to a higher level of TSES elements, where the current level of protection is not sufficient and does not fulfil the function of the TSES element. As with the previous group, the basis for the establishment of this set of proposals is proposed confrontation of maps with the map of the proposed TSES skeleton with the map of positive SEP. Similarly, the degree of protection (from 2nd to 5th) is indicated.
c) *proposal for new protected areas* – proposal for protection and determining the degree of protection for elements of TSES that are currently unprotected, as well as the protection of newly designed TSES elements. The basis of the draft legislative protection is a map of the proposed TSES elements. It must clearly establish what level of protection is proposed and the justification for protection.
d) *proposal for protection of natural resources*, primarily forest and water resources – proposal for the re-classification of commercial forests into categories of forest protection and forest areas specifically designated for inclusion in the TSES by law no. 326/2005 on forests. The proposal to create a category of protective forests is mainly based on interpretations of abiocomplexes, maps of area classification based on abiotic factors. It is also proposed to use this category to include forests located in sensitive areas for the occurrence of geodynamic processes. Specifically, designation of forests with the primary function of nature protection is proposed *especially for forests forming interactive elements within the TSES*. Proposal of TSES elements significantly helps with the legitimate protection of water resources, large-scale protection of water resources in protected water management area, and in basins of water flow. In

PHO of the II. degree according to Law no. 364/2004. There is a positive impact on TSES also from other laws and protection of the thermal and mineral water resources and protection of soil resources.

e) *proposal for cancellation of protection* – a rare proposal where the territory has been assigned legislative protection but now the territory has a low value of landscape, characterised by a high degree of degradation and due to the degree of degradation it cannot fulfil that function. The basis for the determination of these proposals is the confrontation of the territorial classification map and the synthesis map of positive effects.

The final result of this group of measures is the preparation of a *proposal for legislative protection of individual elements of TSES and natural resources.*

Proposal for elimination of stress factors are designed to mitigate the impact of stress factors on the landscape. The map of negative elements in the given territory constitutes the basis for the group of proposal. This group of proposals can be further subdivided into individual measures consisting of:

a) *proposal for new technological measures* to reduce the production of contaminants, especially from the proposal of technological measures to reduce emissions of air pollutants, as well as the proposal of technological measures to reduce pollution of soil, water resources and eliminate sources of noise stress on the environment.
b) *proposal to eliminate sources of stress factors* – is primarily to mitigate the impact, if necessary to remove the primary sources of stress factors negatively affecting various landscape elements.
c) *proposal for revitalisation of areas with environmental loads* – the measures are intended to revitalise individual environmental elements and natural resources.
d) *proposal to mitigate the barrier effect between anthropogenic landscape elements and the elements of TSES*. This group of proposals is based on the map of the proposed skeleton of TSES and the map of negative phenomena in a given territory. The proposal addresses overcoming of these barriers, e.g. when ecological corridors are interrupted by roads which cannot be closed, it is necessary to project tunnels, underpasses or other types of ecoducts as required by the most sensitive species which cross the road. A negative impact of transport corridors is a significant problem for migrating fauna and is responsible for a number of roadkills and injuries. This step is considered the most important, monitored, visible with considerable influence on the general public.

TSES documentation comprises the following parts:

a) *textual part* – contains data on the submission of a project, delineation of a territory, description of analyses, syntheses, interpretations and classifications, evaluations, proposals and regulations for creating a functional TSES.

b) *graphical part* – contains a set of maps with the purpose-arranged contents and combination spatial information. As TSES is a tool primarily addressing spatial relationships, maps are a critical output of TSES.

Because of the continuous supplementing, it is advisable to draft the TSES in the GIS environment.

An adequate arrangement and projection of the results into a map form is a crucial step not only in terms of their presentation, but also a subsequent implementation of the results. The results could be arranged into 3 maps.

a) *Map 1 – The present landscape structure* containing:
   - Representative geoecosystems (REPGES)
   - Physiognomic-ecological mapping units of CLS
   - Protected areas of nature and natural resources.

b) *Map 2 – TSES Proposals* containing:
   - The skeleton of TSES (biocentres and biocorridors) and their protection status
   - Proposal for localisation of non-forest woody vegetation
   - Proposal for ecostabilising measures

c) *Map 3 – Territorial system of stress factors (transparent overlay):*
   - Sources of stress factors
   - Area affected by stress factors, cores and barriers

There are numerous methods, including computers and GIS, which can be employed to produce a graphical representation of the result.

2.2.6 Territorial System of Ecological Stability (TSES) and Landscape-Ecological Planning (LANDEP) within the territorial planning framework in Slovakia

The harmonisation of human activities with the properties of landscape forms a base for the sustainable land use. The purpose of the decision-making process of ecologisation is to determine the limiting indicators (limits and restrictions) resulting from landscape-ecological documentations (landscape-ecological plan, territorial system of ecological stability, etc.) for the localisation and realisation of individual activities.

Determining the limiting values requires an extensive collection of data on the operation of the landscape system as a whole and on its individual components. It is so because the successful and conflicts implementation of every human activity is to a certain degree dependent upon a wide variety of factors in an environment in which the activities are carried out. Therefore the properties of landscape as a whole as well as those of its individual components represent certain limits for the localisation and realisation of individual activities.

TSES, as binding legislative documentation, is a part of the set of land-technical project documentation within the territorial planning process (Act No. 50/1976 as amended by Act No. 237/2000) and must be transformed into the form of ecological regulation of the spatial optimisation of a territory. Pursuant to the law, a regulation of spatial arrangement and functional use of land is a *binding directive,* which guides the localisation and arrangement of a certain structure or implementation of a certain activity in a territory. It is expressed by the values of *characteristics of elements of landscape structure* in words, numbers and, if applicable, also graphically. The regulation has the character of bans, restrictions or supporting factors in relation to spatial arrangement and functional use of the territory. Hereby, the regulation determines forbidden, restricted and allowable activity or functions in a territory (§ 139 of Act no. 50/1976 as amended by Act No. 237/2000). The application of the regulations divides a territory according to the possibility of its use, conditional use, up to strict protection. On one hand, the regulations either restrict or prohibit performance of certain activities, on the other, they allow some activities, they are an offer for utilisation of the area.

Preparing a good set of regulations in relation to the development and application of TSES in planning is a very difficult process. A lot of TSES documents are not processed at such a level that one can easily deduce landscape ecological regulations of spatial development. From this aspect, it is necessary to revise the TSES documentation, and transform it into the form of regulations, and incorporate those in the individual project documents (land consolidation projects, spatial planning, river basin management plans for forest management plans, flood risk management plans). Projecting TSES as regulations into project documentation means that for each area of the territory we define those activities that in terms of TSES it is not possible to site in the given area, which can be localised with certain restrictions, as well as activities that are appropriate and necessary in the TSES.

Based on the above regulations the possible selection of appropriate activities in a given area can guide regional development so that it is to the greatest extent in accordance with the TSES.

The output of this phase of TSES creation is the spatial projection of the TSES elements as regulations with the character of forbidden, limited, and supporting activities.

The aim of the ecological evaluation of the present functional use of the territory is to define those ecologically problematic areas in which the present land use does not correspond with ecological criteria. In other words, to identify the areas where the present land use is restricted by some of the ecological factors. The aim of the newly proposed, ecologically optimum use of the territory is to eliminate these problem areas, to foresee possible new problems and thus to create a spatial structure which is in harmony with the natural and socio-economic conditions of the territory. The ecologically optimum use of the territory is a basic precondition for the sustainable land use (Izakovičová, 2000).

2.3 Strategic Environmental Assessment (SEA) and spatial planning processes

2.3.1 Strategic Environmental Assessment and spatial planning – rational and potential benefits

Spatial planning can be defined in general as an interdisciplinary and comprehensive approach directed towards balanced regional development and the physical coordination of space according to an overall strategy. It gives geographical expression to the economic, social, cultural and ecological policies of society (*European Regional Spatial Planning Charter, CoE 1983*).

Spatial planning refers to the methods used largely by the public sector to influence the future distribution of activities in space and it is undertaken with the aim of producing a more rational organisation of activities in space, including the linkages between them; and to balance development with the need to protect the environment (EU Compendium of Spatial Planning Systems and Policies, CEC, 1997).

2.3.1.1 What are SEA methodological principles in spatial planning?[1]

The need for an early application of SEA in spatial planning is inevitable. The late acceptance of SEA in the planning process often means a limitation to find possible fundamental alternative solutions to the problem (e.g. the project will not be licensed, or it will be without the substantial policy alternatives). The position of SEA in land-use planning practice is clearly expected to balance the weaknesses of EIA applied at project level (Belčáková, Finka, 1996a, 1996b; Belčáková, Finka, 1999).

On regional and local level plans and settlement dimensions, a lot of decisions are taken. These decisions are legally binding for plans on hierarchically lower levels. We should have in mind that, in many countries, sectoral plans have only directive effect for the location of different activities in space. Their realisation is dependent on the decision under spatial planning process.

Referring to a number of experiences, in early SEA step it is necessary to review the environmental carrying capacity of an investment at all planning levels to a maximum degree in order to exclude wrong planning and decision-making steps. Spatial planning measures on regional levels, that are relevant in relation to environmental issues, should be analysed concerning the importance of environmental impact prevention having in mind the scope of relevant detail degree, i.e. planning details.

The project level EIA monitors the environmental consequences of the realisation of a project. Under this process it is not possible to address the heterogenity of intended facilities and uses of land in the interaction with the existing structure. EIA of projects can not ensure the evaluation of cumulative and synergistic effects of different activities in space. This is a dominant role of SEA, namely SEA in spatial planning.

The evaluation of spatial and cumulative effects is expected from SEA and mainly from SEA in spatial planning process, the one which represents inter-sectoral planning. SEA in spatial planning has to point out and address the potential environmental risks and their originators. Namely, regional level seems to be the most appropriate one in order to evaluate spatial and cumulative effects since the region represents an adequate

---

1 Sections 2.3.1.1–2.3.1.3 are based on a presentation at the SEA seminar in Szentendre, Hungary (Belčáková, I., 2004: Strategic Environmental Assessment and spatial planning in Slovakia: Current practices and lessons for practical application of the EC SEA Directive. Available at: http://archive.rec.org/REC/Programs/EnvironmentalAssessment/pdf/seminar2004/Ingrid%20Belchakova_bp.pdf, accessed: June 24, 2018).

spatial unit and since the regional land-use plans are, on the basis of their co-ordination tasks, the place where sectoral plans meet together in many countries.

SEA in spatial planning overcomes the implementation framework of ecology issues in up-to-date practice where the environmental aspect is often presented not transparently without difference between the "description of present state" and "environmental impacts evaluation" as well as without the analysis of feedback of secondary and cumulative effects.

It is difficult to assess the spatial planning measures on regional level by the EIA methods and standard EIA factors, taking into account its characteristics and different levels of details in comparison to concrete project investments and effects.

There is also a different spatial degree and scope of details of land-use planning documentation which is, by its nature, a planning instrument determining the limits of spatial development and which can be a condition of necessity for reduction of the environmental assessment to important aspects of land-use planning solutions.

On the other hand, the assessment of cumulative and synergic effects requires a relatively detailed analysis of space while the analysis suggests the existence of ecological comprehensive model for a region. Thus, complexity or comprehensiveness of EIA is the barrier of the methodological borders of possible implementation. Apart from that, the high complexity can heavily meet the requirements of transparency and effectiveness of the assessment. On the contrary to EIA on project level, at the level of spatial plans the stakeholders of planning developments that would be responsible for financing are usually not known.

Another important aspect not to be neglected is the time. The extent of planning process can reduce the effectiveness of spatial planning actions. The implementation of SEA into a hierarchical decision-making spatial planning system seems to be the optimal solution despite of a number of unresolved questions, i.e. weaknesses.

2.3.1.2 What are the main functions of SEA in spatial planning?

The most important function of SEA in spatial planning is its contribution to a stronger environmental orientation in spatial planning. On one hand, SEA directly joins the process of planning and decision-making, and on the other hand, it can meet those impacts that interfere above the framework of the actual decision-making process.

Further functions of SEA in spatial planning are (Belčáková, 2001):

- SEA in spatial planning helps in the preparation of decisions and has a possibility to bring a great number of information on predicted environmental impacts resulting from planning measures during decision-making process.
- SEA in spatial planning explains the ecological, social and economic context of planning process and can function as a warning in order to protect the environment against already revealed and clearly described dangerous situations and risks together with, what is important on regional level, not clearly described potential dangers.
- SEA in spatial planning has to present information on such environmental impacts which own existence and consequences are not exactly defined.

SEA in spatial planning can, in this way, contribute to an improvement of decision-making process since it is a comprehensive, systematic and transparent assessment of ecological, social and economic aspects and problem implications. The coming conflicts between environmental protection and sectoral interests' requirements in spatial planning can not be solved during the SEA process. These require political solutions that are transformed into decisions about a certain planning alternative. In this decision-making process, SEA can guarantee neither rational decision nor an appropriate consideration on ecological requirements. Its task is to contribute to such decision by its transparency and comprehensiveness. In a democratic society it is hardly possible to neglect or ignore the information on predicted ecological impacts of the developments that is systematically gathered and documented and objectively evaluated.

Thus, SEA in spatial planning has, in relation to a sectoral planning, the function of influencing and mitigation of land-use planning negatives. Its task is to contribute to such planning which is from environmental point of view not only bearable but optimal as well, while at the same time it searches for different alternatives when considering the ecological, social and economic impacts. These are evaluated by appointed value scales, their impacts are related to the best alternative and the possible risks revealed.

2.3.1.3 What are the tasks of SEA in spatial planning?

The main tasks of SEA in spatial planning can be defined as follows:

- To measure the output of which should be the creation of information database for the process of land-use plan elaboration and for the decision-making process in spatial planning by the analysis of ecological, social and economic impacts, i.e. identification, description and evaluation of effects of spatial planning;

- To address alternatives or possible solutions resulting in optimal carrying capacity of land;
- To mitigate negative consequences on the environment.

While defining the subject of SEA in spatial planning, we must have in mind the realisation of spatial planning measures, e.g. decisions that have directly resulted from or have been conditioned by the proved solutions of spatial planning.

Apart from the subject of SEA, the process also comprises the level of "value" (classification, evaluation). Its aim is to come to the evaluation of a proposed spatial planning documentation in relation to expected ecological social and economic impacts. That is why it is necessary to determine criteria and evaluation scales in the form of targets and standards of environmental quality.

The degree to which the environmental evaluation of spatial planning documentation can address the carrying capacity of proposed solutions is dependent on the quality and comprehensiveness of environmental background materials. The evaluation process does not mean that we would like to determine the absolute value of carrying capacity in relation to the environment but we have in mind its relation to a certain defined basic criteria.

The carrying capacity thresholds of such comprehensive environmental system is too difficult to be set up. Apart from that, the issue of environmental quality itself is not an issue that can be determined generally. It is rather a question dependent on scientific knowledge and social targets and, thus, its content is dynamic. It means that also assessment criteria can be static neither in time nor in spatial dimension and it is not possible to establish them unambiguously, through SEA process.

No matter what methods are applied, the social system of values and targets is always the main decisive normative basis. Without this, it is not possible to transform the description and quantification of environmental potentials and factors into their evaluation.

Environmental quality evaluation criteria, being the basis of environmental potential determination, are also a basis of environmental assessment of a project, programme, plan or policy. So it is an assessment of how the realisation of a certain intention can influence the current (actual) potential of the affected area not only in ad hoc but in a trajectory of its predicted spatial development.

SEA can play an important role towards sustainable development.

Sustainability is the common objective for both spatial planning being the planning tool and also for SEA being an assessment tool. It is also assumed that spatial planning and SEA have complementary objectives, that both are instrumental with their aims to achieve sustainable development (Partidario, 2000, Belčáková, 2001).

The connection of spatial planning and SEA is understood as the inevitable condition for acceptable development and an important opportunity for enforcing approaches leading to sustainable development in the decision-making process.

SEA can deliver environmental improveness and raise environmental awareness having a potential to reduce the negative and enhance positive environmental impacts associated with the implementation of spatially relevant plans (Jones et al., 2005)

Furthermore, several years ago some authors defined additional opportunities of SEA in spatial planning with a consecutive summary as follows (Curran et al., 1998, Brown and Thérivel, 2000, Sadler 2001a, 2001b, Owens and Cowell, 2002, Thérivel, 2004 in Jones at al., 2005, Partidário, 2004):

- We may not adequately account for environmental issues without SEA.
- Planners are inadequately informed about the current state of the environment without having SEA.
- SEA can generate consistency and compatibility between the aims, strategies and policies of the particular plan, stressing potential linkages, conflicts and interactions.
- SEA can improve environmental quality of planning policies.
- SEA can raise awareness of environmental impacts.
- SEA can inform stakeholders of the environmental impacts of strategic decisions.
- SEA can help to avoid delays in plan implementation by highlighting how environmental issues have been taken into account during decision-making.
- SEA can identify issues to be monitored during the implementation of plans.
- SEA can improve the green image of planning authorities.
- SEA facilitates the earlier consideration of environmental impacts, the examination of a wider range of potential alternatives, generation of mitigation measures and the potential to address a wider range of impacts.
- SEA has the potential to streamline the EIA process by focusing it on the most significant project issues.

Planning practitioners very often claim that spatial/land-use plans already cover a lot of SEA requirements. Thus, similarities between spatial planning and SEA have been considered against the application of SEA, especially in EU accession countries in the 1990s.

SEA in spatial planning has to present information on environmental impacts without their existence and consequences being exactly defined within the planning process itself.

It is necessary to emphasise the added value of SEA in spatial planning as a facilitator for sustainable decision-making. But we still have to look for the application of appropriate procedural, institutional and methodological framework and for the utilisation of relevant criteria and indicators in SEA in spatial planning – what are still issues under the discussion.

It is widely recognised that spatial planning and Strategic Environmental Assessment (SEA) are prerequisites for achieving acceptable forms of development and that the combination of the two processes can greatly assist decision-makers in working towards sustainable development. There is, however, a continuing debate over the precise role and purpose of each activity.

According to Eggenberger and Partidário (2000), spatial planning integrates environmental, social and economic aspects of spatial development. Therefore theoretical approaches describing individual forms of their integration in spatial planning are intensely matured and on the other hand for relevance of SEA in integrated spatial planning. Taking into account the integration of the above-mentioned aspects is not a new requirement in spatial planning. The innovation of this principle lies in a new vision of integrity in a context of sustainability. It is first of all their mutual influence in the final synergetic quality and not in additive integration (see Table 5).

The issue of flexibility, rationality and integration approaches are the main opportunities of effective SEA in spatial planning.

SEA in the area of spatial planning in most countries is practised at national level, at the level of regions, macro-regions and/or town settlements especially with their local significance in context with the environment that is the subjects of our interest from the aspect of various time periods and positive perspectives, i.e. ad effectum the sustainable development in the given area. (Belčáková, 2015).

The extent to which the requirements for environmental assessment are applied in physical and spatial plans is significantly different between, e.g. the Netherlands and the Nordic countries on one hand and some South European countries on the other. The remaining countries could be found

Tab. 5: Forms of integration

Substantive (technical and methodological) integration meaning: a) the integration of physical or biophysical issues with social and economic issues; b) the integration of emerging impact assessment issues such as health, risks, biodiversity issues with traditional biophysical, social and economic EA approaches; c) the integration of cumulative impact assessment, technological assessment public participation and other such broader approaches in EIA; d) the integration of the different applications, and experiences with the use of particular tools such as GIS, multicriteria analysis and assessment or evaluation (e.g. are we actually being accurate when we assess impacts in the way as determined by a formal multicriteria assessment?); e) the integration of professionals and terminologies in true interdisciplinary teams.
Procedural integration meaning: a) the integration of land-use planning, EIA and resources management; b) the integration of sectoral permitting/licensing processes and EIA; c) the integration of public participation in its various forums (EIA, land-use plans, governmental regulations, permitting processes)
Policy integration meaning: a) the integration of sectoral regulations; b) the integration of sectoral strategies; c) the timing and opportunities of political intervention; d) institutional cooperation.

Based on Partidário (2000)

in various positions between these two groups. The differences are not so visible between the countries but between the various types of physical and/or spatial planning, i.e. between the requirements for environmental assessment on national levels that are adopted by governmental decisions and specific local physical plans that are approved according to precisely defined legal procedures. It means that efficient application of SEA is always tailored to planning needs for better decision-making. In this respect, the so-called tiering aimed at more appropriate identification of issues and alternatives is also a significant factor.

Fischer (2002 and 2007) suggests a systematic application of SEA in planning where systematic decision tiers are frequently synonymous with administrative levels and based on different case studies he reveals different levels of "strategicness" in spatial/land-use SEA.

2.3.2 Evolution of SEA concepts, systems and approaches in spatial planning

The history of formal introduction of environmental assessment of spatial/land-use plans starts in the 1970s. Since then, spatial planning SEA has been formalised in only about 20 countries (Sadler, 2001a). A significant boom that could be witnessed after 2001 may be related to multiple international initiatives, organisations and political decisions.

The very first country officially introducing environmental assessment requirements into public decision-making were the United States by adopting the US National Environmental Policy Act (NEPA) on federal level in 1969. NEPA neither differentiated between SEA procedures and EIA ones nor used the "Strategic Environmental Assessment" term explicitly. It introduced the term EIA as an impact assessment tool of "any major public decisions on new regulations, plans, programmes or projects (Jones et al., 2005, Partidario, 2004). Later, in 1978, the term "major public decision" related also to the area of spatial planning was more precisely defined in Council of Environmental Quality Regulations (CEQ Regulations) in California. The USA is the origin of a methodological approach based on the EIA model called "Programmatic EIA" and EIS for spatial plans. This model is sometimes marked as programmatic, regional, cumulative or generic EIS.

In the 1970s, the USA were followed by Canada (1973), Australia (1974), West Germany (1975) and France (1976). However, methods in none of the countries represented systematic SEA processes.

At that time the development of environmental assessment in spatial planning in EU member countries was influenced by individual EC initiatives. Member countries in successive steps adopted certain formal requirements for environmental assessment of spatial/land-use plans. Nevertheless, there were huge differences between particular countries.

Later, the second half of the 1980s was the period of a dramatic expansion in application of environmental assessment into planning (Wood and Dejeddour, 1992) thus creating relatively well established SEA systems in spatial planning – California, Western Australia, New Zealand, Canada, South Africa, the Netherlands, Italy, Germany, Finland and the UK, that had their unique administrative actions, decision-making levels, formal requirements also in SEA coverage (Fischer, 2007).

Wood and Dejeddour (1989) introduced the term "Strategic Environmental Assessment" in their study commissioned by the EC and the original "EIA of policies, plans and programmes" was transformed into "Strategic Environmental Assessment" as a new methodological tool.

New methodological approaches, more flexible, less quantifiable and more corresponding to the reality of spatial planning were initiated. Each country reacted individually and finally two different approaches could be observed. In expert papers they are referred to as "EIA-based" and "plan-based". The second group reasoned that "SEA should need to perform differently as it has to address level of decision that is considered strategic and more adapted to comprehensive and multiple purposes, forward looking, and uncertain, nature of spatial planning" (e.g. Lee and Walsh, 1992, Therivel et al., 1992, Wood and Dejeddour, 1992, Sadler and Verheem, 1996, Thérivel and Partidário, 1996, Partidário and Clark, 2000, Partidário, 2004). The first group, on the other side, strictly supported the idea that there is no major difference between EIA and SEA.

The EIA-based model is applied mostly in the USA, the Netherlands, Italy, South Africa, California, Germany. Countries like Canada, New Zealand, the UK and the Scandinavian countries prefer the strategic approach (Verheem, 1992). In addition to differences in methodological approaches, there are differences also in terminology due to differences in understanding the content of the expressions "environment" and "strategic". They use different expressions for environmental assessment of spatial/land-use plans, e.g. regional EIA, Strategic Environmental Assessment Analysis, environmental Appraisal of Development Plans, Sustainability Appraisal of Regional Planning, Strategic EIA, Programmatic Environmental Assessment (Partidário, 2004).

The most dynamic expansion in spatial planning SEA in Europe was in the 1990s when the 5th action programme was approved and various draft versions of formal SEA frameworks were elaborated. Mostly, accession countries performed numerous pilot projects of SEA applications in regional development programmes in order to ask for resources from structural funds (e.g. Poland, Hungary, Czech Republic, Slovakia, Slovenia, Estonia, Latvia, Lithuania).

Table 2 illustrates the situation with SEA requirements in spatial planning in EU member states before 2001. As it could be seen, there existed huge differences between countries and individual areas of SEA application. They are mainly in the following issues (Lee and Walsh, 1992, Sadler and Verheem, 1996, Thérivel and Partidário, 1996, DG XI, 1998, Elling 2000, Kleinschmidt and Wagner 1998, Platzer, 2000, ICON 2001):

- Legislative framework of the SEA process;
- The extent of SEA application in individual areas including physical and spatial plans;
- The form of recording Strategic Environmental Assessment;

- The types of information necessary for the EIS;
- Formal requirements for public participation and the process of collecting comments;
- Measures for integration of the results of environmental assessment of policies, plans and programmes into the decision-making and approval processes;

Many authors include also other countries introducing formal requirements for spatial planning SEA – e.g. China, Korea, Norway, NIS countries.

NIS countries (Russia, Belarus, Ukraine, Kazakhstan, Turkmenistan, Armenia, Georgia, Moldova, Azerbaijan, Kyrgyzstan, Tajikistan, Uzbekistan have SEA type frameworks in place, that include SEA elements. But these are based on the system of the State Environmental Review (SER) established in USSR in the mid-1980s together with the so-called OVOS (assessment of environmental impact requirements). Only Ukraine shows a high compatibility with internationally accepted standards (Cherp 2001, Klees et al., 2002, Fischer, 2007).

In case of NIS countries the driving forces behind were mainly international banks (World Bank) and international initiatives (Sofia Initiative).

One of the important milestones in development of SEA systems and approaches was the approval of European Directive 2001/42/EC dated June 27 on the assessment of the effects of certain plans and programmes on the environment (SEA Directive). SEA Directive does not use the expression SEA explicitly. It insists on environmental assessment for all kinds of spatial/land-use plans establishing a framework for future development consent of EIA Directive project, covers SEA for plans requiring assessment under Habitat's Directive, excludes minor modifications to existing plans and programs and small area plans not having significant environmental effects, recognises the concept of tiering, establishes procedural steps like scoping, consideration of alternatives, consultation and public participation, environmental report preparation, consideration of assessment results in decision-making, monitoring, follow-up, consultation and participation, requires also monitoring and consideration of cumulative, synergistic and secondary impacts (Jones et al., 2005).

Dalal-Clayton and Sadler (2005) remark that SEA Directive is probably the best known SEA framework law, and together with the SEA Protocol to the Espoo Convention (UNECE, 2003) it will influence not only the EU countries but it will stand as a "reference point" for countries in Asia, Africa and South America. The biggest influence of the SEA Protocol will probably be seen in the UNECE counties. At the same time it is assumed that the implementation of the Directive could be accompanied by complications, illogicalities and duplications in many land-use planning systems since previous SEA experience and individual land-use planning contexts are often very different.

Partidario (2004), however, remarks that the approved SEA Directive eliminated the effort and expectations for a more planning and policy-oriented evaluation tool, representing a strategic instrument for EU member states. She also mentions that although the Directive is not too strict in whether individual countries should implement it within an EIA Act or as a separate SEA Act or within planning or assessment mechanisms, the Annex 1 exactly defines information necessary for elaborating an Environmental report. This way it clearly represents a highly structured and technically oriented EIA-based model.

EU member states were obliged to implement the Directive by the end of July 2004. In many countries the implementation implied modifications in legislation accompanied by preparation of guidelines. Fischer (2007) mentions that with the exception of Portugal, Greece and Luxembourg the Directive was implemented in all EU countries by June 2006.

The legislative harmonisation of the Directive with the applied formal requirements divided the countries into the following groups (Fischer 2007):

- Explicit SEA framework laws without combination with spatial planning: the UK, Denmark, Spain, Ireland, Malta, Cyprus;
- Explicit SEA framework laws without combination with spatial planning: Finland and Hungary;
- Amendments to existing EIA regulations: Belgium, Estonia, Latvia, Czech Republic;
- Amendments to existing EIA regulations in combination with amendments to land-use planning legislation: Slovakia, Poland and Germany;
- Amendments to an Environment Code: The Netherlands, Slovenia, Italy;
- Amendments to an Environment Code in combination with amendments to land-use planning legislation: Sweden, Lithuania, France;
- Amendments to land-use planning sector: Austria.

Several countries prepared their specific guidelines for spatial planning, comprehensive guidance for spatial planning – e.g. the UK, Sweden, Finland, Denmark, Poland, Ireland and Hungary.

Thanks to the activities of development banks (World Bank), international aid organisations (UNDP, OECD), donor agencies, international activities, there is vast experience with SEA in more than 30 developing countries (Dalal-Clayton, Sadler, 2005).

2.3.3 Best practice and experience, future directions

With gradual increase of SEA application in spatial planning there is a growing number of available case studies and information on best SEA practice and experience. While first European evaluation reports focused mainly on the formal requirements (Lee and Hughes, 1995), more recent spatial planning SEA evaluations consider the evaluation of quality and efficiency in the area by using multiple criteria. For example, Jones et al. (2005) differentiate the so-called process input and output criteria, where process input criteria are represented by evaluations of legal, institutional arrangements and SEA procedures and methods, and process outcome criteria are represented by evaluation of the achievement of identified goals or the contribution to best practices.

Fischer (2007) in his comparative analysis differentiates eleven (11) so-called SEA system context factors (legal requirements, a well-developed legal, political and administrative support base, strong enforcement mechanisms, leading to practice complying with requirements, an independent support environment agency/institute/commission, appropriate funding, time and support for SEA, clearly defined responsibilities), procedural factors (screening, scoping, report, review, summary, monitoring, process integration, consultation, public participation), methodological factors (consideration of appropriate alternatives, clear prediction, minimisation, mitigation, compensation).

During recent years of SEA development, several SEA systems/approaches and several SEA interpretations have been established also in the field of spatial planning depending on different context and political issues, procedural and methodological factors. Till now there have been appeared no unified approach or model among SEA specialists in terms of requirements of complex SEA system. It is obvious that it relates to the different spatial planning mechanisms being very often different in their scope and content. Based upon analysis of different SEA systems it is possible to generalise a complex SEA system as the one consisting of legislation framework, SEA screening requirements, scoping, EIS, public participation and consulting, review, monitoring and/or audit. Concerning the methodological procedures as well as methods, SEA in spatial planning is often closely related to a consideration of environmental/sustainable and cumulative effects as well as the rationality of the assessment process (Belčáková and Nelson, 2006).

In most cases the implementation of SEA requirements are specified within the frame of particular sectoral or spatial planning legislative frameworks. Formal requirements are variable – from ministerial decisions to official regulations at national, regional and local levels. The importance of those three levels differs from country to country and often depends on the degree of centralisation/decentralisation of spatial planning process. The experience gained so far indicate still open unresolved issues in the following areas (Belčáková and Nelson, 2006; Fischer, 2006):

- Limits in the existing planning practise that could slow down the effective integration of SEA approach into this practise;
- Maintaining the application of legally guaranteed tools, mainly at the level of national policies;
- Possible additional costs in the planning process and time delay resulting from SEA application;
- Limits in the existing SEA methods, in information necessary for such assessment and lack of qualified and experienced experts.

From the analysis of SEA examples it is obvious that they were all built on the same basic principles of better decision-making. At the same time they represent many variations in methods of environmental assessment and in individual steps of the assessment process. These differences are mostly linked to a concrete application of environmental assessment within the entire planning process, to individual phases of the assessment within the planning process as well as to different conditions for SEA implementation (Belčáková and Nelson, 2006).

There is a big SEA development now, especially after SEA Directive transposition, what can result in better SEA practice in this field.

Based on case studies authors have identified following areas of possible future developments:

- SEA systems cannot be effectively developed without the knowledge of the wider decision-making system in which they operate.
- We need to know what works and what does not before designing any EIA/SEA systems.
- Incremental reforms may be more effective then their total overhauls.
- Thorough discussions between planners and SEA team are the key for future development.
- Procedures and examples from different context should not be followed blindly.

2.3.4 Landscape planning and Strategic Environmental Assessment – linkages and mutual benefits

The issue of integrated spatial planning and SEA can be viewed as a dual-process: on one hand, the instrumental role that is played by SEA in the integrated planning approaches towards sustainability, and on the other hand, the need to ensure integrated planning for effective SEA. It appears a paradox, but in fact it shows that iterative and reciprocal processes must be put in place simultaneously (Partidário, 1999).

It seems to be necessary to improve our integration capacity by allowing assessment to take place at different levels of decision-making, integrated with other mechanisms, rather than just at the end. SEA can be quite instrumental here, whereas its role would be more towards the influence on the way decisions are made and the ensurance that sustainability values, principles and directions are set, and integrated, right at the outset of any policy, plan or programme, hence affecting its capacity to play the role of a potential sustainability management mechanism.

Landscape planning instruments represent one of the most comprehensive planning mechanisms of landscape protection and development. In this context, implementation of preventive systems can be made considerably easier and can be coordinated with the help of landscape planning instruments and methods.

Environmental assessment is the environmental management instrument which considers and evaluates environmental effects of decisions that are taken into account before these decisions are made. It can be undertaken for individual projects (Environmental Impact Assessment – EIA) and for policies, plans and programmes (Strategic Environmental Assessment – SEA) (Belčáková, 2012).

Environmental assessment tools can deliver environmental improveness and raise environmental awareness having a potential to reduce the negative and enhance positive environmental impacts associated with the implementation of certain projects as well as relevant policies, plans and programmes (Jones et al., 2005).

Landscape planning instruments exist in a number of countries. In most systems these are normally baseline-led instruments that aim at outlining, evaluating and assessing the existing and anticipated status of the landscape, and frequently also of the bio-physical environment for a certain planning area. Frequently, anticipated conflicts and impacts connected with future potential land use are also identified. Furthermore, landscape planning normally deals with the establishment of compensation measures for identified impacts of projects, policies, plans and programmes (Schmidt, et al., 2004).

The main strength of majority of landscape planning instruments is the capability to provide for some comprehensive environmental baseline data for both EIA and SEA, despite of some overlaps.

The connection and/or co-ordination of landscape planning and environmental assessment is understood as the inevitable condition for acceptable development and an important opportunity for enforcing approaches leading to sustainable development in the decision-making process.

Sustainability is the common objective for both landscape planning being the planning tool and also for environmental assessment being a preventive (assessment) tool. It is also assumed that landscape planning and environmental assessment have complementary objectives, that both are instrumental with their aims to achieve sustainable development (Belčáková, 2001; Schmidt et al., 2004).

Environmental assessment can contribute to an improvement of a decision-making process since it is a comprehensive, systematic and transparent assessment of environmental, social and economic aspects and problem implications. The arising conflicts between landscape protection and sectoral interest requirements in planning (mostly in land-use planning) can not be solved within the assessment process. These conflicts require political solutions that are transformed into decisions about a certain planning alternative. In this decision-making process, EA can guarantee neither rational decision nor an appropriate consideration of environmental requirements. Its tasks are to contribute to such decision by its transparency and comprehensiveness. In a democratic society it is hardly possible to neglect or ignore the systematically gathered, well-documented and objectively evaluated information on predicted environmental impacts of developments.

Thus, EA has, in relation to a sectoral, land-use or landscape planning, the function of influencing and mitigating predicted adversities. Its task is to contribute to such planning which is from environmental point of view not only bearable but also optimal, while at the same time it searches for different alternatives when considering environmental, social and economic impacts. These alternatives/impacts are evaluated by appointed value scales, their impacts are related to the best alternative and the possible risks revealed.

It is necessary to emphasise the added value of linking environmental assessment and landscape planning as a facilitator for sustainable decision-making. But we still have to look for the application of appropriate procedural, institutional and methodological framework and for the utilisation of relevant landscape/landscape ecology criteria and indicators in EA – what are still issues under the discussion.

And, also, it is widely recognised that landscape planning and environmental assessment are prerequisites for achieving acceptable forms of development and that the combination of the two processes can greatly assist decision-makers in working towards sustainable development. There is, however, a continuing debate over the precise role and purpose of each activity.

The issue of flexibility, rationality and integration approaches are the main opportunities of effective EA in relation with landscape planning.

Several authors remarked that landscape planning instruments/landscape ecology instruments exist in a number of countries (e.g. Austria, France, Germany, Ireland, Italy, the Netherlands, Spain, Sweden and Switzerland) serving as baseline-led instruments that aim at outlining, evaluating and assessing the existing and anticipated status of the landscape, and frequently also of the bio-physical environment for a certain planning area (Herberg, 2000; Joao, 2004; Sheate et al., 2004). In these countries, instruments are designed differently, e.g. in terms of their objectives, legal status and scope of application.

The extent to which landscape planning requirements are applied in environmental assessment are significantly different between the EU countries. The differences are visible on the various aspects of landscape considerations in the assessment, i.e. between the requirements for environmental assessment. It means that efficient application of environmental assessment is always tailored to meet the needs of better decision-making.

There is a big environmental assessment development now, especially after EIA/SEA Directives transposition and ELC implementation, what can result in better practice in this field.

Landscape is one of the environmental characteristics that is specifically identified in the above-mentioned EC Directives focusing on environmental assessment. Others include human health, biodiversity, fauna, flora, soil, water, air and cultural heritage.

Landscape along with other environmental topics are often used to form the basis of EA objectives. EA objectives and related indicators provide a measure against which the effects of the project or policies, plans and programmes can be assessed.

In EU member states, based on the EC Directives it is now a legal requirement to consider the interactions between all environmental factors.

There are many overlaps regarding the contents of an EIA/SEA environment report and regional and local landscape plans, particularly regarding the collection of environmental baseline data, the outline of environmental objectives and the assessment of the likely significant effects of the proposed plan on the environment.

On the other hand, landscape planning instruments can function as a comprehensive information source for SEA, potentially helping to save time and resources and reducing the efforts connected with producing an SEA. The greatest potential of landscape planning instruments lies in the collection and evaluation of environmental baseline data, as well as the setting up of environmental objectives. Furthermore, the methods used within landscape planning can also be used within SEA. Landscape planning also contributes to the development of mitigation measures.

Table 6 illustrates that landscape planning instruments can contribute to varying extents to a number of EA elements. It indicates that each instrument has different strengths and weaknesses.

Early years of EA application saw the development of numerous methods designed to ensure that various stages of the EA process were carried out in a comprehensive and systematic way. In the context of project EA, e.g. checklists and matrices were developed for pinpointing potential direct impacts. Networks were found to help consider indirect impacts. EA methods should allow to organise information and be beneficial for practitioners with limited experience. The most frequently used EA methods are listed in Table 7. Whilst the use of assessment methods and techniques would normally be left to the discretion of practitioners, they may also be prescribed in regulation or guidelines. EA methods and techniques will differ, according to the sector and tier of application. SEA of a regional land-use plan, e.g. will require the application of different methods and techniques as an EIA for a road (Belčáková, 2008).

The assessment of cumulative effects is an aspect of EA that requires particular attention. A range of methods are available, from the more analytical matrices, to the planning oriented multicriteria analysis (Smit, Spalding, 1995; Sadler, Verheem, 1996; in Belčáková, 2012). The majority of existing methods considers impacts only upon one aspect of the environment, e.g. a single species. The nature of assessment at strategic level, however, means that it is more appropriate for methods to focus upon area wide effects rather than upon details of the proposals. Generally speaking, the assessment of cumulative and synergistic effects requires a comparatively detailed analysis of space. In this context, e.g. the ecological comprehensive regional development model introduced by Westman (1985).

Tab. 6: Possible contribution of landscape planning to EA elements

Country	Legislation	Objectives	Contents	Possible contribution to EA elements
Germany	Federal Nature Conservation Act 2004, (comprehensive landscape plans at all planning levels)	- sustained availability of the natural resources for human use - integration of considerations of nature and landscape into decision - making (especially in terms of spatial planning)	- existing and anticipated status of nature and landscape - principles of nature conservation and landscape management - assessment and evaluation of the existing and anticipated status of nature and landscapes, possible conflicts - measures for avoiding, reducing or eliminating adverse effects on nature and landscapes - measures for protecting, managing and developing certain parts or component of nature and landscape	- strong contribution in provision of baseline data - significant contribution to impact assessment and preparation of compensation measures - indirect contributions to alternatives assessment, public participation and monitoring
Slovakia	Act on Town and Country Planning and Building Code (comprehensive landscape plans ar regional and local levels)	- optimal spatial arrangement of human activities based on landscape ecological conditions	- landscape ecological analysis of landscape elements and factors - syntheses of landscape ecological characteristics - interpretation of landscape conditions - ecological optimisation of land use	- strong contribution in provision of baseline data - significant contribution to impact assessment and preparation of compensation measures - indirect contributions to alternatives assessment, public participation and monitoring

Scotland	No formal requirements, (Landscape character assessment – Guidance for England and Scotland)	– landscape character assessment as a reference point in policy, plan and programme formulation – to inform decisions about change and development, so they are consistent with landscape objectives	– digital landscape character types database – provides a baseline against which change can be monitored and to inform decision making – identification of critical areas – visualisation of the results for use in potential management regimes – recommendations regarding mitigation and design considerations	– strong contribution to impact assessment – Some contribution to monitoring and public participation – Indirect contribution to compensation measures
Sweden	No formal requirements (ecological landscape plans)	– sustained availability of natural resources	– existing and anticipated status of natural resources and landscape – principles of nature conservation and landscape management including health aspects – assessment and evaluation of the existing and anticipated status of nature and landscapes, possible conflicts – measures for avoiding, reducing or eliminating adverse effects on nature and landscapes – measures for protecting, managing and developing certain parts or component of nature and landscape – implementation of health aspects	– strong contribution in provision of baseline data and impact assessment – some or indirect contribution to alternatives assessment, compensation measures and public participation

Source: based on: Hoppenstedt, A., 2004, Schmidt, M. et al., 2004, Žigrai, F., 1996, Swanswick and LUC, 2002, Mörtberg U.M. et al., 2007, in Belčáková, 2012)

Tab. 7: Methods used in EA

Types of methods	Relative usage	
	EIA	SEA
Analogs	H	L
Checklists	H	M
Decision-focused checklists	M	L
Environmental cost benefit analysis	L	O
Expert opinion	H	M
Expert system	L	O
Indices or indicators	M	M
Laboratory testing	M	NA
Landscape evaluation	M	H
Literature reviews	M	L
Mass balances	H	L
Matrices	H	M
Monitoring (baseline)	L	O
Monitoring field	L	O
Networks	M	O
Overlay mapping	M	H
Photographs/photomontages	M	L
Qualitative models	H	L
Quantitative models	M	L
Risk assessment	L	L
Scenario building	L	L
Trend extrapolation	L	L

Notes: H – high usage, M – moderate usage, L – low usage, O – limited usage, NA – not applicable
Source based on Canter, Sadler, 1997; Belčáková, 2008

The most commonly used landscape planning/landscape ecology methods and techniques for impact analyses and assessment are listed in Table 8.

Landscape planning methods are all useful for environmental assessment procedures, especially for baseline data collection informing on the current state of biodiversity, nature and environment or identification of aims and objectives and evaluation of potential conflicts. They can work as a beneficial mechanism to describe, analyse and compare environmental effects. One of the frequently used landscape planning method in EA is a so-called ecological risk analysis where environmental impacts are as-

Tab. 8: Landscape planning methods and techniques used for impact analysis and assessment

Type of method	Description
Scenario analysis	scenarios are used for projections to outline and compare means and conditions of the implementation of a proposed action based on reasoned assumptions
Computer modelling	used for calculation of impacts of strategic actions on environmental indicators (e.g. habitat supply analysis in Canada and the USA)
GIS	useful for assessment of cumulative effects of several projects in the same area
Ecological risk analysis	assessment of strategic risks, regarding trends that may undermine objectives and quality standards generating potential relevant damages and costs
Compatibility analysis	analysis and assessment of compatibility of different alternatives
Sensitivity analysis	analysis and assessment of policy options using factors of common analysis that enable an interpretation of sensitivity and effectiveness
Forecasting and simulation	analytical calculation or simulation of potential changes generated by the development of actions and the consequent potential impact of strategic options
Carrying capacity	good for setting development thresholds according to the sensitivity of the environmental and social systems. This method is useful in the assessment of cumulative impacts and sustainability thresholds

Source based on Canter, Sadler, 1997; Haaren et al., 2008

sessed for a number of factors and interrelations between them. Factors should be identified, described and evaluated.

In addition, landscape ecology provides methods and tools for addressing effects on landscape scale, such as effects of habitat loss and fragmentation, e.g. ecological modelling and other GIS based tools (Piscová, et al., 2011; Mörtberg et al., 2007).

Furthermore, overlay maps are commonly used for the preparation of plans and, also, they can be used for the assessment of environmental factors in order to identify environmental conflicts. In order to resolve conflicts, GIS based scenarios for site alternatives are developed, e.g. regarding residential developments.

Landscape indicators that are based on pressure-state-response framework have been quite often used within the framework of the so-called Landscape Heritage Assessment (LHA) and Landscape Characterisation Assessment (LCA), especially in England, Scotland, Wales and Ireland.

Indicators need to be targeted on measurable attributes. In this context, it is possible to define landscape characteristics that are measurable in a qualitative if not quantitative way. Landscape is taken to include both countryside and townscapes. Indicators need to provide a good indicator of change in character, have resonance (capture public attention), be capable of measure and use meaningful data. The setting of objectives, targets and indicators should take place as part of the scoping stage of EIA/SEA before baseline surveys are completed.

Following the analysis of landscape planning instruments in selected European countries, it is suggested that landscape planning can make a significant and beneficial contribution to EA.

The main strength of all landscape planning instruments is the capability to provide for some comprehensive environmental baseline data for both EIA and SEA. Furthermore, all instruments can contribute extensively to impact analysis and evaluation, the assessment of alternatives, identification of compensation measures, public participation and monitoring.

A range of landscape planning and/or landscape ecology methods are readily available for impact prediction and evaluation. These range from methods and techniques that are applied frequently over those that are used moderately to those that are limited according to specific landscape planning context.

During recent years of EA development, several EA systems/approaches and several EA interpretations have been established depending on different context and political issues, procedural and methodological factors.

In most cases, the implementation of EA requirements are specified within the frame of particular sectoral or comprehensive planning legislative frameworks. Formal requirements are variable - from ministerial decisions to official regulations at national, regional and local levels. The importance of those three levels differs from country to country and often depends on the degree of centralisation/decentralisation of landscape planning process.

The experience gained so far indicate still open unresolved issues in the following areas:

- limits in the existing planning practise that could slow down the effective integration of EA approach into this practise;
- maintaining the application of legally guaranteed tools, mainly at the level of national policies;
- possible additional costs in the planning process and time delay resulting from EA application;

- enhancement of the scope of landscape planning in order to improve the support of EA;
- promotion of a better integration and co-ordination of strategic action, landscape planning and EA;
- testing the practical application of contents and methods of landscape planning within EA in form of pilot projects;
- awareness raising of the strength of landscape planning in order to overcome the missing political will and to promote formalised landscape planning approaches.

It is obvious that both - landscape planning and EA procedures were built on the same principles of better decision-making. At the same time they represent many variations in methods and in the individual steps of the assessment process. These differences are mostly linked to a concrete application of environmental assessment within the entire planning process, to individual phases of the assessment within the planning process as well as to different conditions for EA implementation.

3
Practical application – case studies

Erika Kočická, Ingrid Belčáková,
Andrea Diviaková, Eliška Belaňová

3.1 SEA of Bratislava Master Plan[1]

3.1.1 Introduction

Part of the decision-making process at the level of the local land-use plan of Bratislava, according to the Act of the Slovak National Council No. 127/1994 on EIA, has been to carry out the assessment that is of the strategic environmental assessment character. There is neither official methodology for the SEA adopted yet nor any rules determined by legislation for the SEA process (there are SEA provisions in EIA Act, but very general ones, there is no SEA executive regulation). This case study can be considered as the voluntary SEA process. The city of Bratislava initiated it in order to increase the quality and acceptance of the plan as well as the involvement of the citizens to implement the intentions of the local plan and to make the process to be more democratic. On the other hand, this project is to prove a new methodology of the SEA implementation in land-use planning that was carried out in co-operation of the two universities and planning practice.

The spatial development plan of Bratislava is very demanding since the assessed plan is in detail the land-use plan at the local level, but the territorial scale is at the regional level (the scale of development plan at the regional level). The process of strategic environmental evaluation has been executed when 3 draft variants of blue print land-use plan had been available. Public had the access to the written, table and graphic parts of it. Moreover, the subject of assessment is not only the actual plan but also the strategic documents that have been used as the basis for its elaboration, because these have not been a subject to the SEA process before.

The aim has been the integrated assessment of all the aspects of the proposed spatial development plan in relation to meeting the objectives of sustainable development and its enforcement at the level of the city of Bratislava. The process of SEA has been implemented as an integral part of the planning preparation process that safeguards the optimal existence of feedback as well as implementation of the results of the SEA process in selection and elaboration of the final variant (3 variants). After the completion of

1 This section is largely based on a presentation at the SEA seminar in Szentendre, Hungary (Belčáková, I., 2004: Strategic Environmental Assessment and spatial planning in Slovakia: Current practices and lessons for practical application of the EC SEA Directive, available at: http://archive.rec.org/REC/Programs/EnvironmentalAssessment/pdf/seminar2004/Ingrid%20Belchakova_bp.pdf, accessed: June 24, 2018).

the SEA process, Ministry for the Environment of the Slovak Republic published their official standpoint on the SEA process outputs and issued some "instructions" based on the environmental assessment results.

Among the key actors or stakeholders were local authority of Bratislava, SEA professionals (2 EIA Centres were involved), Ministry for the Environment, NGOs and Bratislava citizens. Bratislava city authority was the responsible body.

Mainly *substantive, methodological and procedural forms of integration* were achieved to a certain extent.

Physical, biophysical, social and economic issues as well as the emerging issues such as health, risks, bio-diversity and climate change had been integrated before SEA process started. But the integration level was not very evident. In the written part of all three alternatives of Bratislava spatial plan the goal of sustainable development has been stated. But this general statement has not been detailed in different spatial planning aspects of the plan.

Basically two main aspects of methodological integration between the SEA process and spatial development plan elaboration have been used:

a) the strategic evaluation of spatial development plan goals and aims in different aspects towards sustainability principles and criteria (sustainability test);
b) quite detailed Bratislava spatial plan evaluation when, also, cumulative assessment played a key role.

Cumulative impacts were identified in order to "prescribe" potential problem areas to be solved at the hierarchically lower level of Bratislava land-use plan - zone level. So this may be seen as the adoption of co-ordination, co-operation and subsidiary as guiding principles for spatial planning at different levels.

As far as the procedural form of integration concerns, we would like to stress the very successful integration of *professionals in a truly interdisciplinary team and the affected stakeholders in the decision-making process.*

Institutional and policy forms of integration are still falling behind.

The SEA process has formally been initiated before the decision on the all three variants of the plan has been done but parallel with the planning process.

3.1.2 Procedural and methodological aspect

The SEA of Bratislava land-use plan has followed the already existing legislative framework represented by the EIA Act, namely its article 35 on SEA and by the Land Use Planning and Building Order Act. There were three alternatives of the Bratislava Land Use Plan. The SEA took place before the final decision of Bratislava Land Use Plan had been taken.

The SEA document comprised the written, table and graphic parts.

Assessment procedure:

Step 1a): comparison between strategic development objectives included in the Comprehensive Development Strategy of Bratislava City and strategic development objectives included in the individual variants of Bratislava Land Use Plan;

Step 1b): the links between the strategic aims of the development included in Bratislava Land Use Plan and the principles of the so-called sustainable development test.

The following principles have been taken into consideration:

Principle 1: changes in behaviour to meet the needs of the future generations,

Principle 2: social justice and equity in the city of Bratislava, its surroundings and within the Bratislava region (inter-generation, intra-generation and inter-regional solidarity),

Principle 3: responsibility for development of the city of Bratislava, with respect to the future generations rights,

Principle 4: changes in value orientation in relation to cultural heritage, cultural and social identity, education and upbringing,

Principle 5: changes in behaviour and standpoints in reaching the high and stable level of economic growth and employment, in accordance with sustainable development,

Principle 6: changes in behaviour and value orientation in relation to the environment, mainly to its natural components and resources,

Principle 7: changes in organisation and management of public administration, with the emphasis on competences, efficiency and transparency of management, (on the principle of subsidiarity and the integrated principle),

Principle 8: changes in behaviour and standpoints to the international co-operation and securing of global safety.

Step 2: Comprehensive assessment of environmental quality

- evaluation of present state of ecological stability and ecological diversity
- evaluation of present state of quality of hygienic and safety characteristic of environmental elements

- evaluation of present quality for subjective and individual needs
- evaluation of cultural and symbolic quality + evaluation of changes in the above-mentioned evaluations, this evaluation of changes will become a basis for the identification of positive and negative impacts of individual plan policies as well as for cumulative impacts and impact interactions

Step 3: Selection of criteria for environmental evaluation of individual plan policy

- criteria and indicators of the so–called global sustainability as well as local environmental quality:
- reduce overall demand for resources
- efficient use of non–renewable resources
- increase the use of non–renewable resources
- increase the re–use and recycling of resources
- maintain biological diversity
- energy efficiency
- mitigate the possible effects of greenhouse gases
- reduction of pollution effects
- maintain the ecological stability
- nature protection
- maintain the less ecologically sensitive areas
- maintenance and improvement of cultural and historical values
- improvement of overall quality of life
- ensure the socio–economic requirements
- increase community awareness and involvement
- improve equality of opportunity
- ensure the awareness of international projects
- enforce the development of human resources
- create opportunities for local communities to take care of their environment

Step 4: Selection of individual plan policies to be evaluated

- housing areas
- production (industrial, agricultural, ...)
- administration areas
- commercial areas
- non–commercial areas
- social infrastructure
- sport and leisure areas

- transport infrastructure
- water supply system
- sewage system
- energy supply
- telecommunication infrastructure
- nature protection
- landscape design

Evaluation of individual plan policies of all three alternatives - evaluation of their impacts on:

- broader policies
- settlement inhabitants
- natural environment
- urban structures
- landscape
- specific impacts

Step 5: Mitigation measures

- for hierarchically lower levels of land-use planning and for EIA of projects

The outputs of the assessment process where summarised in written, table and graphic parts of the Environmental Assessment Report.

3.1.3 Final remarks[2]

The process of the SEA contributed to the fulfilment of the basic task of spatial planning that is the optimal utilisation of the local area potentials and to enforce sustainability of spatial development of the settlement in its social, natural-environmental, ecological and economic dimension. The process of the SEA helped to reveal the cumulative and synergic effects of implementation of the development intentions included in the local development plan, the conflicts of interests in the territory and reveal possible socio-psychological barriers in acceptance the development intentions in the local plan. At the same time it enhanced the information of the citizens and ensured transparency of decision-making of the respective bodies of self-government, who are fully responsible for adoption of the plan.

2 This section is largely based on a presentation at the SEA seminar in Szentendre, Hungary (Belčáková, I., 2004: Strategic Environmental Assessment and spatial planning in Slovakia: Current practices and lessons for practical application of the EC SEA Directive, available at: http://archive.rec.org/REC/Programs/EnvironmentalAssessment/pdf/seminar2004/Ingrid%20Belchakova_bp.pdf, accessed: June 24, 2018).

Among the crucial element for the successful implementation of an integrated planning approach were participation, formal and informal procedures as well as the appropriate methodological aspects.

The experience of the implementation of the SEA in this case study shows that it is inevitable to ensure the closer institutional, legislative, policy and financial co-operation of the land/use planning processes and the processes of the SEA.

If there is an objective of the active environmental creation in the terms of sustainable development, spatial planning is the one which ensures the realisation of appropriate legal environmental tools. Spatial planning makes balance or harmony within sectoral policies and other interests in the territory including environmental protection and conservation in order to meet sustainable development.

On the other hand, the opposition of planners against SEA was conditioned by the lack of knowledge about this Act or they had not read it carefully. This Act does not prescribe that the spatial planning documentation of regions and settlements are a subject of the whole assessment process but it says that this documentation should contain the evaluation of the predicted impacts on the environment and, also, it should contain mitigation measures.

It is necessary to ensure the appropriate integration of SEA and spatial planning processes, what can endanger neither the function of supplement mechanisms in the form of SEA nor the role of spatial or land-use planning being the optimisational instrument of the relation man–nature and the instrument of management, co-ordination and control of activities in space.

By optimal integration we can avoid:

- limitation of EIA' s function being a control mechanism;
- the opposition against SEA among spatial planning professionals.

In the context of case study, the whole process of SEA has been implemented in the high financial and time pressure and was implemented by the experts that have been working without any financial reward. They were not part of the team that was preparing the plan and their start in the whole process was relatively late and not in right relation to the length of the time the other team members could use for elaboration of their issues. The whole process was complicated by the amendment of the Act on Land-Use Planning that has been approved in the period of creation of this local development plan. It actually meant that there had been an absence of the executive rules and methods during the process of elaboration of the spatial development plan.

Several implications for future actions should be stressed:

- To make the integration of SEA and spatial planning processes more efficient, the integration has to be initiated in the very beginning of spatial planning process, at the stage when spatial plan goals are being established, not at the stage where the draft plan is already available. On one hand, it happens before the final plan is issued but on the other hand, once the aims of the plan are set in a way that they do not reflect the sustainability as a general goal, then it is difficult for SEA to improve the decision-making process effectively.

- SEA should be linked to the tiered approach at the different levels of spatial planning not only in the form of procedural link but also in the form of methodological link. It means that different level of detail and relevant data should be employed for each appropriate spatial planning level.
- Sustainability goals that were determined in Bratislava city development strategy were too general to be effectively detailed in local land-use plan without having completed Local agenda 21.

3.2 Example of ecological carrying capacity assessment for landscape in Environmental Impact Assessment

3.2.1 Introduction

Legislation on EIA (Environmental Impact Assessment) in many cases requires the assessment of the proposed activity from the perspective of carrying capacity of the affected territory. These aspects should be considered (at minimum) during every compulsory process of EIA. The case study is an example of the framework determining the ecological carrying capacity (ECC) in assessing EIA in a model example.

3.2.2 Starting points and terms of reference of ecological carrying capacity assessment

Over the past decades, the issue of *ecological carrying capacity (ökologische Tragfähigkeit)* has drawn the attention of several environmentally oriented research projects as well as the fields of natural (landscape ecology, physical geography), social (sociology, economic, philosophy) and technical (land planning) sciences. The object of interest in assessing capacity is the territory used, e.g. in land-use planning, in landscape-ecological assessment the term *"landscape"* is used.

Ecological carrying capacity is generally understood as a multi-faceted feature of the landscape, integrating the assessment of the natural landscape as well as human society and its creations, because probably only such a comprehensive approach can reveal the true characteristics of the landscape.

Thus far, despite the relatively widespread problems of developing ECC, there is *no uniform methodology for assessing carrying capacity* as such, or partial carrying capacity, or even the content of all steps of the ECC evaluation process. The *terminology is also not entirely clarified*, in many cases, even the very meaning of the various terms used (Kočická, 2004). ECC expresses the *measure of the acceptable (suitable) use of landscape* by anthropic activities, without disturbing and/or destroying natural features, processes and relations between elements of the landscape and even the quality of the environment. ECC is understood as the suitability of using the territory. One instrument for determining the capacity for using the landscape is ecological/environmental limits (Hrnčiarová et al., 1997).

Addressing ECC takes different forms depending on whether this refers only to the carrying capacity of the natural environment or also the anthropogenic part of the landscape. In the existing literature addressing the issue of carrying capacity, we meet with differing natural carrying capacity (natural environment) and social or sociological carrying capacity (social environment), also referred to as human carrying capacity. Many authors, however, in terms of methodological approaches distinguish three basic types of carrying capacity, namely the natural (biophysical) carrying capacity, social (behavioural) carrying capacity and ecological, also known as human, functional, spatial or environmental, depending on the focus of research.

In Slovakia, *carrying capacity* is discussed primarily with the ecological carrying capacity approach (also on the basis of the requirements of the original Law no. 127/1994 on Environmental Impact Assessment). The current law (Law no. 24/2006 on Environmental Impact Assessment and on the amendment of certain laws, as amended – the EIA Law) requires the process of compulsory assessment of evaluation of investment plans to also include preparation of an assessment report on carrying capacity (Annex 11 to the EIA Law).

For correct evaluation of the ecological carrying capacity of the landscape in Slovak conditions it is appropriate to apply the methodology of Hrnčiarová et al. (1997), or its modification (*ECC methodology*). ECC methodology uses determining factors of vulnerability, defined in the work of Roberts (1991). Algorithmically it is based on the principles of the LANDEP Landscape-Ecological Planning methodology (LANDscape Ecological Planning) (Ružička, Miklós, 1982b).

3.2.3 Example of determining ecological carrying capacity in the process of Environmental Impact Assessment

In the *model territory* in the area of Tižinka in Vrátna Dolina valley (cadastral area of Terchová, district of Žilina), ECC was evaluated in the context of the *assessment report* (Kočická, Nikolov et al., 2012) for the proposed building structures (project documentation developed by Ihnatišinová et al., 2011, 2012) at the request for the scope of assessment, issued by the Disctrict Environmental Office of Žilina.

The purpose of the proposed investment project was the *construction of recreational structures for individual family and group year-round recreation* in the rooms and in two-bedroom apartments in the ski area of Starý Dvor - Tižinka (see Fig. 7 and 8). The project was designed with two versions of implementation. The first option (version 1) is 21 buildings - family cottages of two types (type 1 and type 2). The second option (version 2) expects the construction of 25 buildings - 21 family cottages (types 1 and 2) + 4 apartment buildings (apartment buildings 1 to 4), whereby under this version it was intended to also provide in the apartment buildings, in addition to accommodation services, restaurant services and services of a commercial and sporting character (conference rooms, office space, lobby bar, information centre, playground, restaurant with kitchen, a café with a pastry shop, a wellness centre with gym rental and ski service, rental and

Fig. 7 Visualization of the proposed buildings - apartment buildings 1 – 4 (Ihnatišinová et al., 2012)

Fig. 8 Visualization of the proposed buildings - family cottage type 1 (Ihnatišinová et al., 2011)

servicing of bicycles, sports equipment shop, clothing shop, folk art product shop, grocery store, wine shop, and chemist's).

The request for assessment of the carrying capacity of the territory in question arose as part of the approval for *land-use planning documentation* - in the positions on Alteration and Amendment no. 2 ÚPN-SÚ Terchová which was addressed at the time. The stated aspects could be processed, e.g. in the general building scheme of tourism for Vrátna Dolina which was planned.

The carrying capacity of the territory was determined as per the assessment report (Kočická, Nikolov et al., 2012) under Chapter C. II. 17. "The overall quality of the environment - synthesis of positive and negative factors," from which we have taken the text of the following chapter.

3.2.3.1 Location of the assessed activity and nature of purpose of the affected area

The potential for the affected area for the development of recreation and tourism is enormous, considering its wide range of characteristics. In particular, the nature and landscape are attractive and appealing. Socio-economic conditions are also attractive. For these reasons, in this area there is great interest in sports and recreational use (see Fig. 9 to 12).

The territory in question also has the prerequisites for the development of highland agriculture with an emphasis on traditional forms of soil management. Forestry has a rich tradition and high economic efficiency in the wider area.

Due to the existing natural values rich in natural formations, the preserved forest and non-forest communities, important and protected species

Fig. 9 Location of the site in the spatial context of the Vrátna ski resort (http://www.vratna.sk)

and habitats in the same space at the same time, there is interest in the protection of nature, landscape and natural resources; so this area is among the most valuable for conservation and not only from a national perspective but also from the European point of view.

Fig. 10 Location of the proposed facilities in broader context (www.freemap.sk)

Fig. 11 Situational sketch indicating the location of the proposed facilities (http://www.vratnavillage.sk

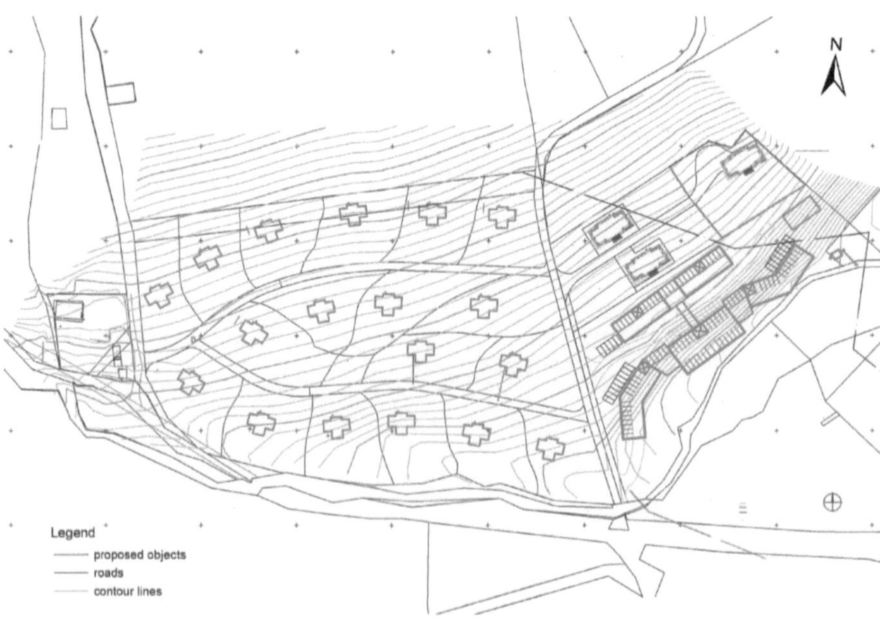

Fig. 12 Situation of the proposed structures (Ihnatišinová et al., 2012)

Fig. 13 – 14 View of the land in question (with the beginning of construction of several structures) from the southwest, from the road to Príslop (Ch. Nikolov, May 2011; Š. Ridoško, December 2012)

Fig. 15 View of the land in question from the opposite slope – Paseky ski run, with the Vrátna – Starý Dvor centre in the foreground (Ch. Nikolov, May 2011)

The affected area has the character of a slightly rugged hill-country, a channel is eroded by the flow Varínka, surrounded by rugged georelief of an upland to mountainous character with protruding rock formations (debris from the massifs of Veľký and Malý Rozsutec, Boboty and Sokolie). The parcel in question lies at an altitude of 630-650 m asl, the slope has a linear-concave shape, and it is south facing, with an incline of 10°. It also features loam-deluvial stony sediments with modal cambisols. No occurrence of geodynamic phenomena was shown.

The direct affected location of the proposed investment at the time of the assessment report was unused grassland. The riparian vegetation along the watercourse was made up of trees such as *Acer platanoides, Acer pseudoplatanus, Padus avium, Salix caprea, Salix fragilis, Salix glauca, Sambucus nigra.*

Fig. 16 – 18 Current state of the affected locality (Ch. Nikolov, March 2017)

On the terrain edge above the level of the stream were species such as *Corylus avellana, Crataegus monogyna, Euonymus europaea, Fraxinus excelsior, Padus racemosa, Picea abies, Rosa canina, Salix sp., Swida sanquinea, Tilia platyphyllos, Ulmus glabraa* and more. The herbaceous layer was represented by species such as *Arctium tomentosum, Calamagrostis arundinacea, Geranium phaeum, Geum rivale, Hypericum perforatum, Mercurialis perennis, Petasites albus, P. hybridus, P. kablikianus, Rubus caesius, Senecio nemorensis, Silene inflata, Taraxatum officionale, Urtica dioica* and others. Using report of the Malá Fatra National Park (NP), the paper by Stanová, Valachovič (eds.) (2002) on the basis of field inspections and the presence of indicator species identified the occurrence of the habitats Br 6 (Riparian Petasites 6430) and Lk1 (Lowland hay meadows 6510). The incidence of more significant species was not shown; the habitat was in a degraded state.

Due to the need for environmental impact assessment of construction on the environment, the recommendations of the Malá Fatra NP report led to targeted fieldwork on selected animal species: birds and amphibians (Flajs, May 2012) and small mammals (Hlôška, June 2012). The Malá Fatra NP report provided relevant information on large carnivores (especially the brown bear (*Ursus arctos*), as well as the lynx (*Lynx lynx*) and grey wolf (*Canis lupus* L.). The area also has numerous species of avifauna as *Dentrocopos leucotos, Pyrrhula, Certhia familiaris, Columba palumbus, Aegithalos caudatus, Motacilla cinerea, Phoenichuros ochruros, Dryocopus martius, Phylloscopus sibilatrix, Cinclus, Ficedula albicollis, Picus viridis, Picus canus, Dendrocopos major, Dendrocopos minor* and is also visited by *Strix aluco, Falco peregrinus, Falco tinnunculus, Accipiter nisus, Accipiter gentilis, Aquila chrysaetos, Scolopax rusticola, Aegolius funereus, Buteo, Corvus corax, Pernis apivorus, Nucifraga caryocatactes, Aegithalos caudatus, Jinx torquila, Muscicapa striata*; above the area we can see *Tetrastes bonasia*, we can assume a lekking ground is here. The location is a hunting ground for several species of birds of prey. It is also a breeding ground for *Lanius collurio* and *Saxicola rubetra*. It is used as a feeding site for several species of thrush (*Turdus merula, Turdus philomelos, Turdus pilaris, Turdus torquatus, Turdus viscivorus)*. The edge of meadow is also used for nesting by the Tree pipit (*Anthus trivialis*). The amphibians observed at the site were *Salamandra salamandra* and *Rana temporaria*. Reproduction of those species was not confirmed. Monitoring small mammals recorded occurrences of four species from the order of rodents (Rodentia): *Apodemus agrarius, A. flavicollis, Myodes (Clethrionomys) glareolus, Microtus (Pitymys) subterraneus*. Movements of bears, lynx or wolves were not registered on the site.

The area in question is located in the Malá Fatra National Park, in zone C, in an area with the 3rd degree of protection under Slovakia's Law no.

543/2002 on the protection of nature and landscape as amended. From the European network of protected sites, the site in question is within the Malá Fatra protected bird area (SPA). Habitats of European importance in the Natura 2000 system (Sites of Community Importance - SCI) in spatial relation to the site in question are Malá Fatra and Varínka. The area is part of the protected water conservation area (WCA) of Beskydy and Javorníky. In the wider surroundings of the area of interest, several sites have been identified which represent areas significant for the territorial system of ecological stability (TSES) known as the "skeleton" of the TSES (see Fig. 19.-21. The landscape scenery of the site in question is dominated by calcareous cliffs.

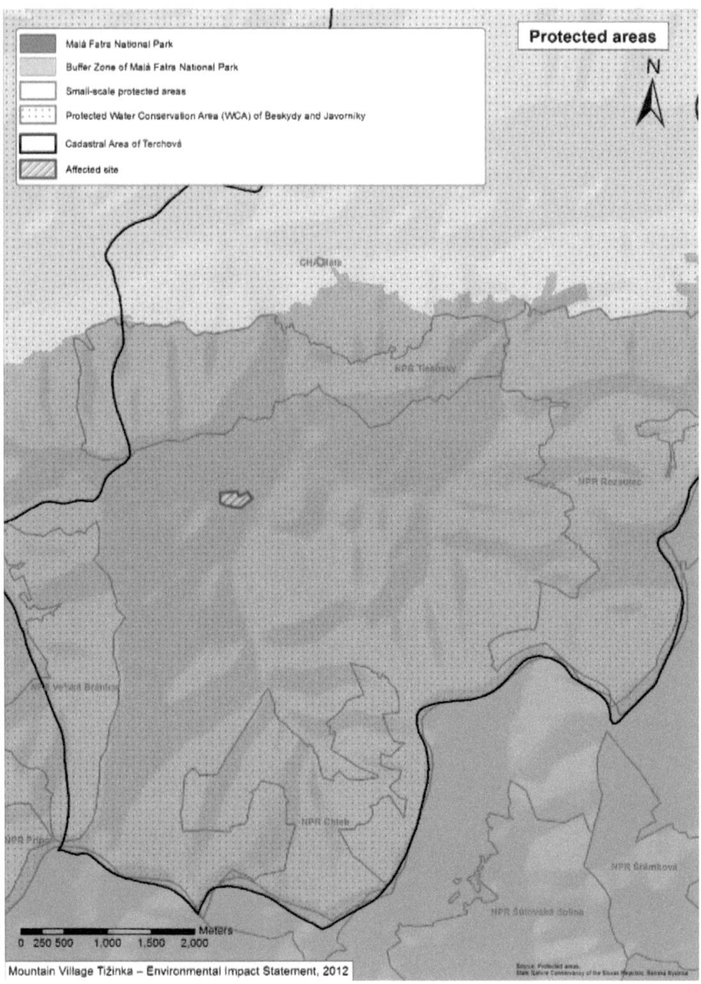

Fig. 19 Protected area in national network of protected areas (www.sopsr.sk

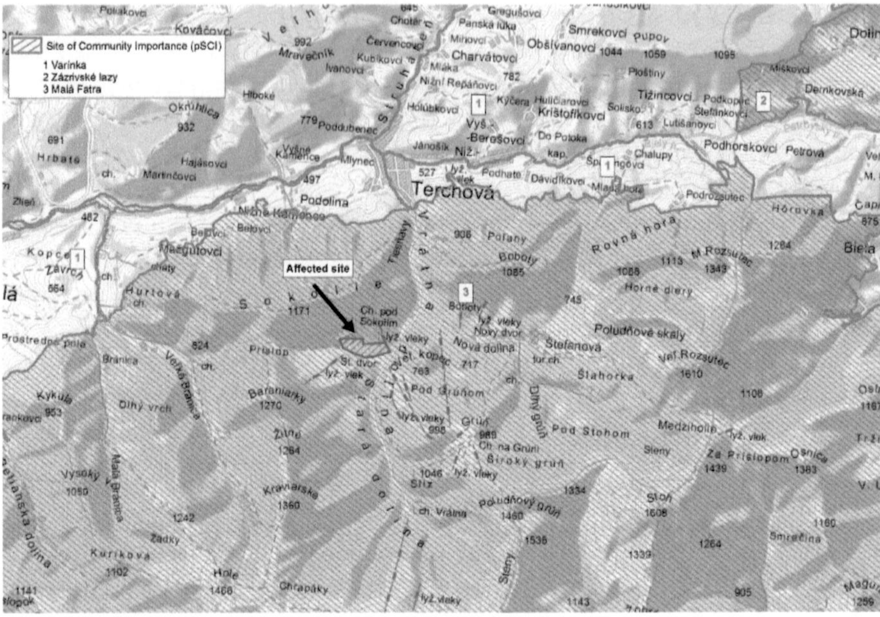

Fig. 20 NATURA 2000 protected area -Habitat of European Importance (www.sopsr.sk)

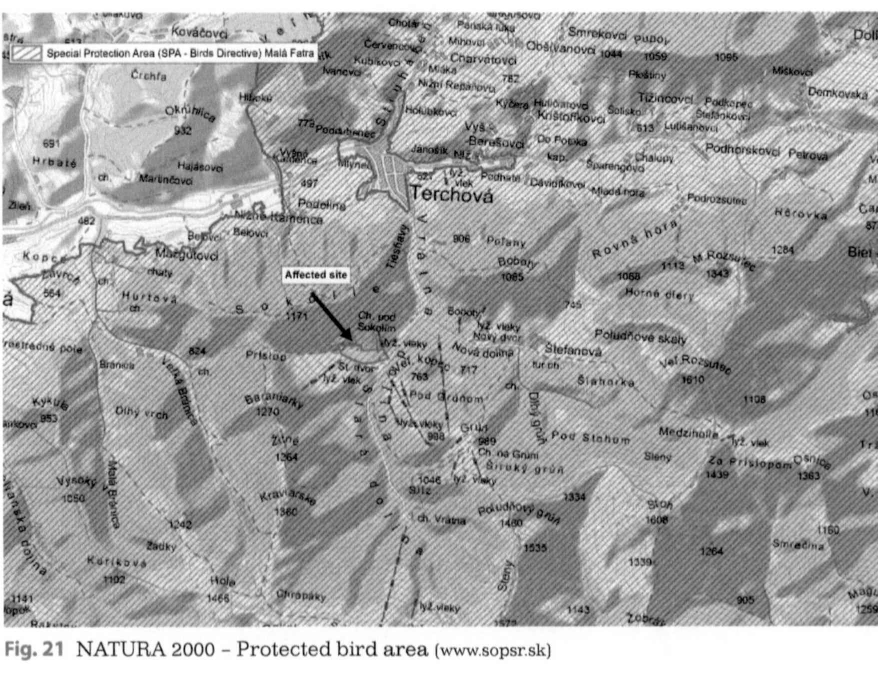

Fig. 21 NATURA 2000 - Protected bird area (www.sopsr.sk)

The territory is without undisturbed environmental quality. The coefficient of ecological quality of cadastral area, according to the Landscape Atlas of the SR (Miklós, Kočická, Kočický In: Miklós Hrnčiarová (eds.), et al., 2002) is in the range of 0.61–0.8%.

3.2.3.2 Visitor numbers for the affected territory

Visitor numbers to Vrátna Dolina have been monitored by Malá Fatra NP (formerly PLA) continuously over about two- to three-year intervals since 1976. It monitors the frequency of vehicles in the Tiesňava area and also the frequency of visitors to sites Snilovské sedlo, Medziholie and Podžiar sedlo that are prominent nodes in hiking trails, was well as the top of Suchý peak. Monitoring takes place during the summer season, in the months of July-August, during different days of the week. The same methodology is used at the same locations to aid comparability of results. According to the obtained outputs (internal materials of Malá Fatra NP administration) the highest daily attendance in the reporting period was achieved in the year 1988 - 5770 visitors, average attendance seen was 5260 visitors (see Tab.9. and Tab.10). The visitor numbers up to that time were also very high. A sharp decline in the number of visitors occurred during the year 1988 due to the closure of the campground in Vrátna Dolina due to overloading both of the camping (not meeting sanitary requirements), but also the whole valley. The campground could accommodate 1,000 people, in tents, in caravans and cabins. After the closure of the camp, visitor numbers halved.

Tables documenting summer visitor number for the monitored period of 1976–2012:

Tab. 9: Maximum visitor numbers found for Vrátna Dolina for the monitored period 1976–2012

Year	1976	1980	1982	1986	1988	1992	1998	2001	2003	2004	2006	2009	2012
Maximum visitors	5467	5713	5284	5680	5770	2395	2837	2778	4294	2827	2931	2484	3445

Source: Kružliaková (2012)

Tab. 10: Average visitor numbers found for Vrátna Dolina for the monitored period 1976–2012

Year	1976	1980	1982	1986	1988	1992	1998	2001	2003	2004	2006	2009	2012
Average visitors	4075	3801	4512	4835	2217	1814	2096	1919	2389	2072	2467	2213	2259

Source: Kružliaková (2012)

In terms of movement along the hiking trails there have been no significant changes from the past, the numbers have different values at all locations (ranging from 0 visitors per day – Snilovské sedlo – Chleb in 2012 to 1,486 visitors per day – Snilovské sedlo – Veľký Kriváň in 1986), with no pattern.

From the results of the other two monitoring activities as of the date of the assessment report (Sibilová 2009; Kružliaková, 2012) it was shown that the weather had a clear impact on visitor numbers, with higher visitor numbers during nice weather. Higher numbers were recorded before weekends and during weekend days. Vrátna Dolina is therefore sought after by visitors who want short weekend trips or day trips. These results correspond to the results from 1985 (Demianová, 1985). The monitoring at the time also recorded the catchment area; most visitors were from the immediate surroundings (Žilina, Dolný Kubín, Považská Bystrica), but also from other parts of Slovakia, especially Bratislava, Trnava, Dunajská Streda, with representation of visitors from Moravia and Bohemia (Ostrava, Brno, Blansko and Prague), followed by Germany (GDR and FRG) and Hungary. There were sporadic visits from Poles, but also visitors from the Netherlands, France, former Yugoslavia, Romania and Italy.

In the winter season 2008/2009 Vrátna Dolina was visited by 120 000 people, and there were plans to increase this to 150 000. Visitor numbers in the winter season have traditionally peaked at the end of December (27–31.12.). Visitors are primarily Slovaks, particularly locals and from western Slovakia. Foreign visitors are mostly Czechs and Poles (http://nasazilina.sme.sk).

In the period of highest visitor numbers (the 1980s), the territorial plan for the Malá Fatra and the territorial planning documentation for the zone of Terchová, Vrátna Dolina stipulated a maximum capacity of beds in the former Malá Fatra PLA of 650. The actual number of beds in 1984 was 3120, which by 454 beds exceeded the expected numbers for the year 2000 (2666).

In the period of preparation of the assessment report, the average number of visitors was 2259, which is half that of the 1980s. The current capacity of accommodation facilities in the valley, according to the statistics office for Terchová amounted to 1117 beds (we had assumed that the number was higher). The construction of the assessed activity (205 accommodation bed under the "bigger" option 2) would mean 1322 beds.

3.2.3.3 Approach in determining the ECC of the affected area

Correct determination of the ECC of the territory requires, under the ECC methodology to assess the vulnerability (or sensitivity) of the territory, the ecological significance of the territory and the current (real) burden on it by stress factors.

The ECC methodology has the framework structure of LANDEP methodology, e.g. in the form of the following steps:

landscape-ecological analysis

- *Analysis of elements of primary landscape structure* (PrLS) - primarily (geo)relief, geological-substrate complex, soil;
- *Analysis of the elements of the current landscape structure* (PLS) - land cover, land use;
- *Analysis of ecological and cultural priorities* - protected elements, TSES elements, important elements of the landscape, etc.;
- *Analysis of stress factors* – pollution, degradation, devastation, damage to the biota, soil, water, noise, restricted zones of technical elements, etc.

landscape-ecological synthesis

- *Abiotic (ABK) and landscape-ecological complexes* (KEK)
- *Types of present landscape structure* (types of PLS)
- *Types of ecological and cultural priorities* (types of ECP)
- *Types of current burden on the landscape* (types of CBL)

landscape-ecological interpretation

- *Vulnerability of the landscape*
- *Ecological (and cultural) significance of the landscape*
- Real burden on the landscape

landscape-ecological evaluation

- *Abiotic, biotic and socio-economic limits*

landscape-ecological proposal

- *Degree of ECC*
- *Proposal for ecologically sustainable landscape structure*

3.2.3.4 Assessment in the presented approach took place using significantly simplified modification of the ECC methodology

Vulnerability of the territory is determined by the vulnerability of the individual elements of the landscape. Under the above-mentioned ECC methodology it is interpreted as a property that expresses the vulnerability of the landscape to various *external disturbances* (e.g. permeability of soil, erodibility, gravitational movements, changing water tables, eutrophication, habituation, pollution, destruction of vegetation, etc.). It does not talk about the actual burden, but the potential vulnerability (which can simultaneously be real too).

The georelief and the rock environment of the wider area are vulnerable to various processes of slope modelling, such as slipping, falling and rolling of rocks, avalanche processes and other processes of slope modelling. A common phenomenon in this area is soil erosion caused mostly by water. According to the map of designated survey and landslides areas, the immediate area is not affected by landslides, although in the Terchová cadastral area there are several landslide areas recorded. There is local waterlogging and soaking. The land area of interest is mostly without vegetation cover and is prone to rapid surface and line water erosion, there is a strong deluvial area affected by gully erosion. There is no significant wind erosion in the wider area due to the configuration of the terrain and land cover. Erosion affects mostly deforested areas, since the vulnerability of the soils, apart from relief, rock and actual soil properties is also affected by vegetation cover and land use. Most of the surface of the given non-forest area is grassland, which is critical to soil degradation processes (in addition to reforestation) optimal use, as grasslands have high soil-protective erosion functions. The threat of erosion processes is not whole-area, it is limited to hiking trails, nature trails, the ski slopes, recreational settlements, i.e. places with high visitors numbers. The stated disturbing factors have the character of natural hazards. More negative than natural hazards, there are also anthropogenic threats in this area in particular forestry practices, movement of visitors – trampling of vegetation, soil compaction, land construction and the arrival of more technical structures (transport, infrastructure, sports facilities, lifts and so on.) and their accompanying phenomena (land use, air pollution and water damage to flora, fauna habitat damage, interference with fauna, noise, dust, air pollution, waste management, as well as consumption of water, raw materials, energy requirements, proliferation of non-native species, etc.).

The biota is vulnerable mainly due to farming methods in the area (forestry, agriculture, water, recreation, urbanisation, as well as conservation and management of activities). This can cause mechanical damage and destruction of vegetation, habitat, but also is a source of disturbance of wild fauna and affects their behaviour. Endangerment of wild plants and plant communities has many causes, the most important factor, however, is the destruction of their natural habitat.

The vulnerability of the area in question was assessed in the step, landscape ecological interpretation, in relation to relevant processes and to surface water erosion, gully erosion and waterlogging, or soaking. The vulnerability was defined within the borders of the abiotic complexes in the working geoecological map (map of the primary landscape structure, see Fig. 22).

The abiotic complex (abiocomplex, ABC) is generally a quasi-homogeneous spatial unit in respect of all the considered parameters of all proper-

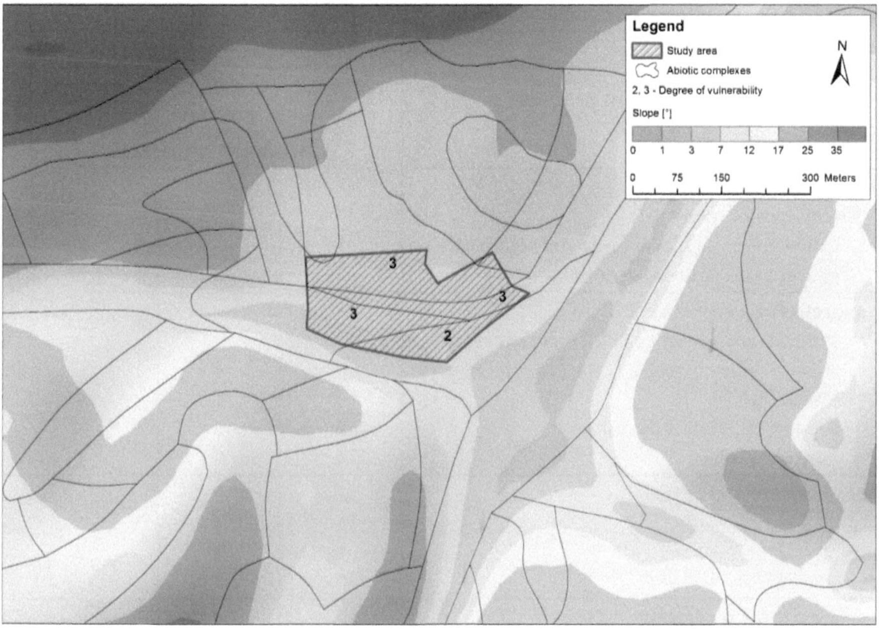

Fig. 22 Simplified map of the primary landscape structure with assigned degree of vulnerability

ties to be considered as part of the abiotic elements, the primary landscape structure (PrLS), as well as the processes and phenomena taking place within the borders of these units. Its homogeneity gives complex units of the same type the same assumptions for the behaviour of the processes within them and the same conditions for social use, making these units the most widely used spatial database information for most applications of landscape-ecological research. The construction of abiocomplexes (and other geosystem units) is based on a systematic approach to landscape (*landscape as a geosystem*) (Miklós, Izakovičová 1997; Miklós, Kočická, Kočický, Diviaková, 2015).

In assessing the vulnerability, the following properties of the abiotic complex were considered (see Tab. 11):

- rock environment – genetic type of rock;
- (geo)relief – morphographic-genetic-position type of (geo)relief, slope and geometric form of relief;
- soil – soil subtype and granularity of soil (soil type).

The stated ABC properties were evaluated in relative increments (on a 5-point scale, where 1 = not at all to moderately vulnerable area, 2 = little-vulnerable area, 3 = moderately vulnerable area, 4 = very vulnerable area, 5 = extremely vulnerable area) as follows:

Tab. 11: Assigned degrees of vulnerability

Indicator of ABC property	disturbing factor		
	water erosion	gully erosion	waterlogging/soaking
	Degree of vulnerability		
Rock environment			
genetic type of rock			
gravel-loam to gravel proluvial sediments	1	1	4
gravel-loam deluvial sediments	2	3	2
georelief			
morphographic-genetic-position type of relief			
slope of valley overall	3	4	3
alluvial fan	1	1	4
slope at the foot of the hill	2	3	3
transport slope	4	3	1
gradient of relief			
3° – 7°	1	1	3
7° – 12°	2	2	2
12° – 17°	3	3	1
geometric form of relief			
concave-linear	2	2	3
linear-linear	2	2	2
Soil			
soil subtype			
modal cambisols	3	3	2
granularity of soil–soil type			
dusty-loam soil	3	3	2

Source: Kočická et al. (2012)

The resulting vulnerability was determined by simple arithmetic mean using auxiliary calculations in worksheets, weighting was not applied, fractions were rounded to the nearest whole number from .5 upwards.

On the basis of the above, overall vulnerability of the affected area was determined as a moderately vulnerable area (3rd degree) with potential disturbing influences (note: the specified level does not reflect the stresses or environmental significance of the area, these special-purpose properties are entered into the determination of ecological carrying capacity below).

The vulnerability of the landscape in the next step is represented by abiotic limits on land use. The vulnerability of biota is usually evaluated separately and represents the biotic limit (here, biota vulnerability has not been considered separately, given the occurring habitats and species of flora and fauna, the area have, in terms of biotic vulnerability, been rated at 2nd degree).

Ecological significance is a feature of the landscape that provides a measure of securing positive ecological processes and functions in the country. Ecological significance means those elements of the landscape creating favourable conditions for the functioning of the processes in the ecosystem and to preserve and maintain favourable conditions for the regeneration and restoration of genetic resources, biodiversity and ecological stability in the country and the restoration of natural resources.

The input for the assessment of ecological significance is the details of the legislative designation of protected areas, species and habitats (species, territorial protection, national, Natura 2000), development of environmental systems, natural resources (forest, soil, water), important landscape structures (historical, unused aesthetic, part of the landscape), the present landscape structure (i.e. land use). (see Tab. 12).

In assessing ecological significance, the following elements of landscape cover were considered:

- forests;
- non-forest tree and scrub vegetation (NTSV);
- permanent grass and grassland;
- water courses;
- grounds of recreation facilities (accommodation and entertainment structures);
- transport and technical structures, lines and surfaces.

The ecological significance of the site in question was determined in the step *landscape ecological interpretation* in the present landscape structure working map, taking into account information on the spatial differentiation of ecologically important parts of the country (see Fig. 23).

The ecological significance of the site in question was determined by the relative scale system (in a 5-point scale, where 1 = ecologically most important territory, 2 =ecologically very important territory, 3 = ecologically moderately significant territory, 4 = ecologically insignificant territory, 5 = ecologically least significant territory) as follows:

The resulting significance was determined by simple arithmetic mean using auxiliary calculations in worksheets, weighting was not applied. Fractional values were rounded to the nearest whole number from .5 upwards. The overall significance of the area came out as an ecologically very important area (grade 2). The ecological significance of this area is also very high according to the Landscape Atlas of the Slovak Republic (Miklós, Hrnčiarová (eds.), et al., 2002), very large.

Real burden expresses the occurrence of all stress factors on the landscape. The burdens on the area Malá Fatra include buildings for accommo-

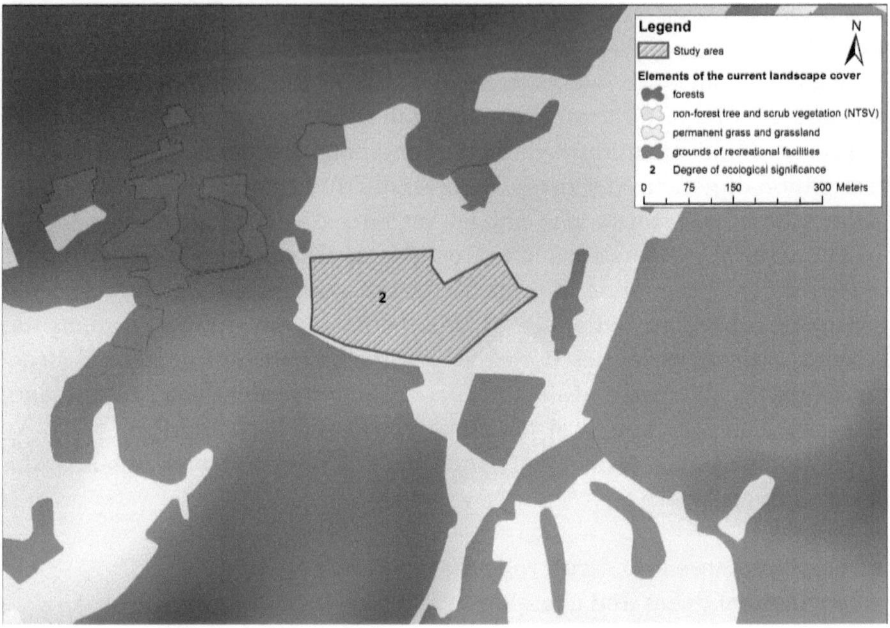

Fig. 23 Simplified map of the current landscape structure with assigned degree of ecological significance

dation, catering and service facilities of varying nature, the network of roads, parking areas and lay-bys, forest and field roads, technical structures of ski lifts, cable cars, sport grounds, forestry, water management, agricultural facilities, hiking trails, etc. Constantly increasing anthropogenic pressure can be observed, using aforementioned natural potential of the landscape, particularly of a recreational character. The stated primary stress factors are complemented by secondary stress factors – intangible and deterioration phenomena. Together, they form the *territorial system of stress factors* (TSSF). The stated activities have varying nature, scale, appearance and impact on the landscape, from small, from traditional farming based facilities, to spectacular projects of hotel complexes. All activities using the natural recreational potential of the area are acceptable activities in this respect acceptable. The question is, however, what is the permissible, tolerable rate of utilisation of the potential, not regarding individual buildings but of the whole wider area. There could occur saturation of the territory with construction of facilities of a similar nature (there are opinions that such a state has already occurred), and exponential spread with many accompanying phenomena negatively affecting the environment of the area.

The general contamination of the soils of the area involves, to the great-

Tab. 12: Assigning degrees of ecological significance

Character of territory	Degree of ecological significance
Legislatively defined territories	
Malá Fatra NP	1
Malá Fatra SCI	1
Malá Fatra SPA	1
Habitats Lk1 and Br6	1
Beskydy and Javorníky WCA	1
Territorial system of ecological stability	
BBc Krivánska Malá Fatra	1
RBk Varínka	3
Natural resources	
forest resources	1
soil resources	2
water resources	1
Important landscape structure	
Sokolie	3
Elements of the present landscape structure	
Forests	1
non-forest tree and scrub vegetation (NTSV)	2
permanent grass and grassland	2
water courses	1
grounds of recreational facilities (accommodation and facility buildings)	4
transport and technical buildings, linear surfaces	5
Rocks	1

Source: Kočická et al. (2012)

est degree, the occurrence of natural soil contamination under risk elements of geochemical anomalies, the impact of global emissions coming mainly from foreign sources and reflected in an increased content of Cd, Pb, Cr, As, the influence of national resources with local and regional impact, resulting from different types of metallurgical and other industries, as well as heating plants, agricultural impact (in particular the Cd content of phosphate fertilizers), and the impact of emissions from vehicles.

The quality of the surface water and groundwater of the wider area is affected mostly by industry. The biggest polluters are industrial companies, water companies (wastewater treatment plants) and landfill and the actual settlements that do not have sewage systems, and therefore discharge waste water directly into waterways. The general pollution is caused mainly by agricultural production. The largest share is primarily crop production through the use of fertilizers and various protective chemical agents (herbicides, insecticides, etc.), which burdens the soil cover, vegetation and groundwater. Pollutants reach watercourses indirectly through infiltration into groundwater and flushing of contaminated soil. These sources include agricultural buildings with inadequate storage of fertilizers, leaking urea tanks, silage troughs and so on. Pollution is linked to farmyards and is linked not only animal excrements, but also to filling stations, which are typically in a critical condition. A minor source of pollution, but even more dangerous, is landfills that are not protected against the leakage of landfill water into the soil and then into surface waters. Typical of this are household waste dumps on the banks of rivers. The bedrock in some places is polluted for decades, in many cases the old environmental burden is in the geological environment in quaternary sediments. In the affected areas these do not occur, as the area is not affected by the above negative phenomena. The Water Act (NR SR Act no. 364/2004 on Waters) defines sensitive and vulnerable areas, which were established by Government Regulation 249/2003 on 26 June 2003. The site concerned cannot, under those regulations, be identified as sensitive or vulnerable regarding water resources.

The dispersion study prepared (Hamza, 2012) identifies the main local sources of air pollution of the assessed area to be transport (the road into Vrátna Dolina valley from Terchová), suspension and resuspension of insufficiently cleaned roads, heating and forestry-agricultural activities (see Fig. 24). The study further states that in the area under consideration pollution levels for hourly and daily values do not exceed the limit values set for the protection of health.

Transport, especially its intensity, is also a major source of noise and vibrations (acoustic studies – Brodniansky, Machlica 2012), where the study states that the noise situation of the affected site during the preparation of the assessment report did not exceed noise limit values in terms of impact on health or the population (see Fig. 25).

In the area there are no dominant or other landscape elements that would have adverse effect in terms of landscape scenery, landscape character and image. On the contrary, there are important landscape features that are natural landmarks (peaks, rocky limestone cliffs – the closest is Sokolie, continuous forests). In the wider area of Terchová there is the characteristic historical landscape structure – terraced landscape with a patchwork of fields, meadows and pastures and vegetation with line vegetation at the edge of terraces. In the affected area such forms do not occur.

The population is exposed to the effect of negative environmental factors, such as pollution or air, water, soil, biota damage, as well as noise, light, odour,

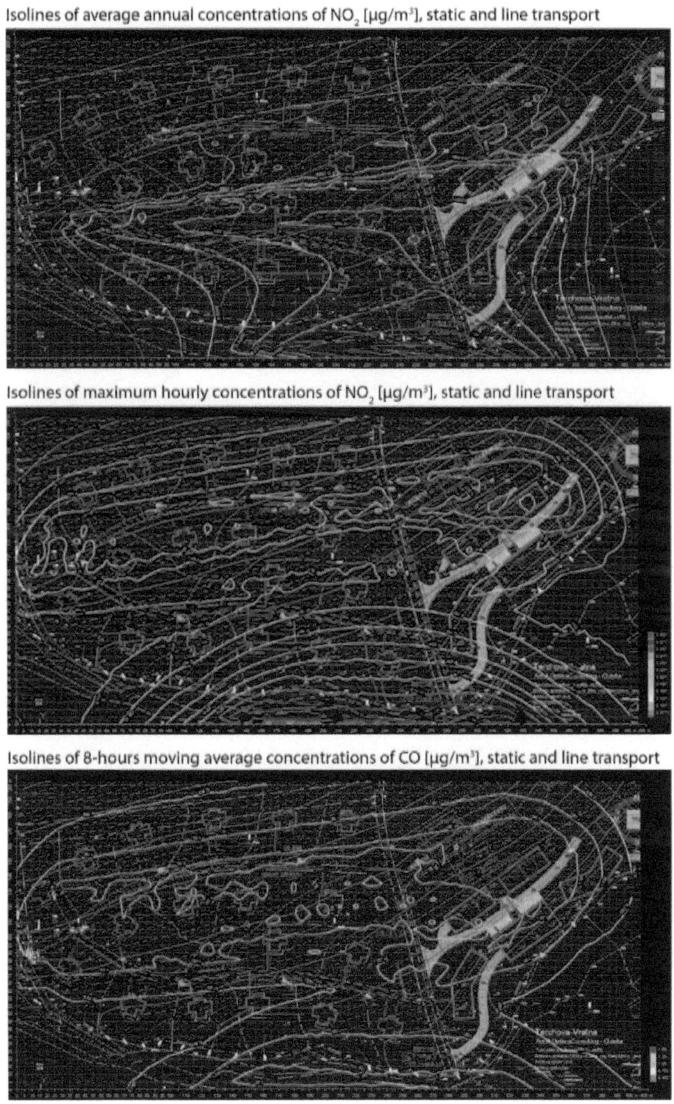

Fig. 24 Emission relations of the affected area (Hamza, 2012)

visual impact, general discomfort, etc. The health condition of the population suggests that these effects are no significant.

In the affected area during the period of the assessment report, primary stress factors were the construction of several recreation facilities consisting of family huts and transport and technical infrastructure in the form of access roads and utility distribution. Secondary stress factors were air pollution emissions from traffic, noise, dust, the occupation and devastation

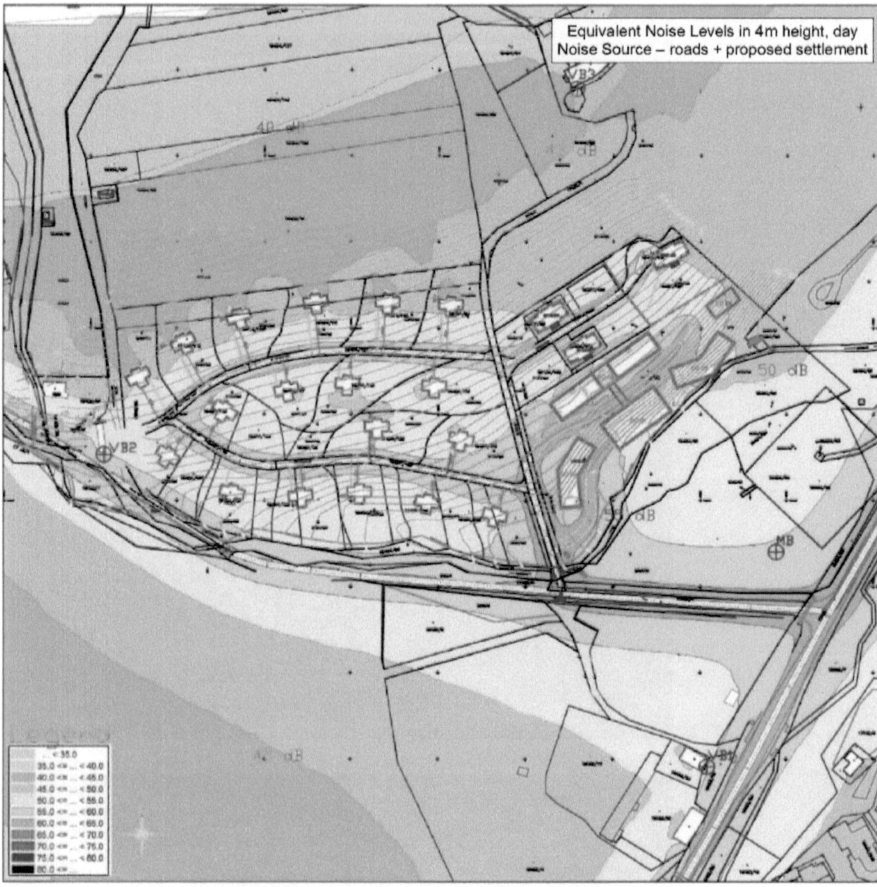

Fig. 25 Noise conditions of the affected area (Brodniansky, Machlica, 2012)

of land, devastation of vegetation and habitats and disturbance of animals, movement of persons and the defined protected areas and buffer zones. The site concerned was territory of a more or less (semi) natural character; the TSSF in the affected area represented a sparse network of structures with unremarkable negative aspects. There was also spatial overlap with elements of TSES. The limited area declared protected and otherwise important territory and elements of a PLS character of stress factors were considered in the evaluation of ecological significance. The most significant deterioration of the relevant phenomena was the subject of assessment under the stated expert studies (acoustic and dispersion). On the basis of the results of the stated assessments, the monitored negative phenomena were shown to be below the limit as well as current and the predicted situation with the existence of the proposed structures. The real burden is presented by the socio-economic limits, in this case, for the above reasons, the real burden of the site concerned does not act as a limit for the intended use of the area.

Ecological carrying capacity was therefore determined in the step *landscape-ecological evaluation* as a combination of the level of vulnerability and degree of ecological significance. The evaluation was carried out in the auxiliary cross table (see Tab. 13), ECC was determined within the boundaries of the ABC on the working geoecological map

Tab. 13: Assigned level of ecological carrying capacity

Significance Vulnerability	1	2	3	4	5
1	1	1	2	2	3
2	1	2	2	3	3
3	2	2	3	3	4
4	2	3	3	4	5
5	3	3	4	5	5

Source: Kočická et al. (2012)

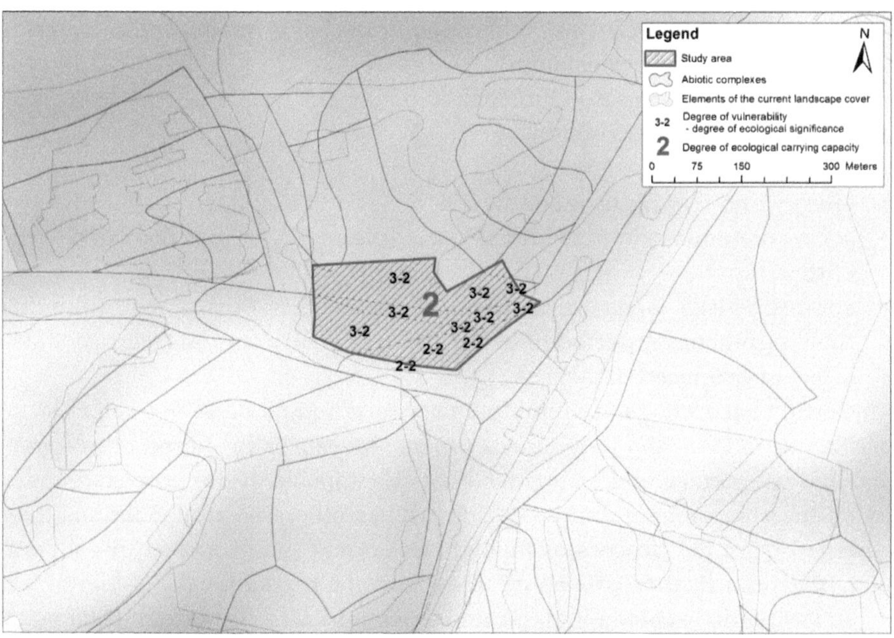

Fig. 26: Simplified map of the Ecological Carrying Capacity

Ecological carrying capacity of the landscape was determined on a 5-point scale: 1 – territory of high capacity, 2 – territory of close to high capacity, 3 – territory of medium capacity, 4 – territory of low capacity, 5 – territory of no capacity.

The resulting level of ecological carrying capacity of the affected locality was determined as level 2, which means territory of close to high capacity (see Fig. 26).

Interpreting the above steps for the needs of assessment of the siting of proposed buildings was performed in the step landscape ecological proposal as follows: in places with ECC = 5 proposals are excluded, in areas with ECC = 3-4 are proposals are limited and in places with ECC = 1 to 2, proposals are possible.

3.2.3.5 Using of the results of ECC assessment in the presented process of EIA

From the stated assessment, for the needs of assessing the possibility of construction of the proposed structures in the assessment report it was shown that the *assessed building structures* in the territory in question, in terms of the carrying capacity of the affected area *can be sited* in both versions (alternatives) considered.

The choice of the most suitable version may be decided by *other criteria*; the assessment report considered:

- the number of proposed building structures;
- area taken by construction;
- number of parking spaces;
- energy and raw material demands, method of heating;
- socio-economic relations and impacts (planned services provided, benefit);
- comprehensive negative impacts of the activity on the environment, their significance, period of action, temporal and spatial synergy;
- effect of proposed measures.

Certain restrictions (and limitations) are *proposed measures* referred to in chapter C IV of the assessment report "Measures proposed to prevent, eliminate, minimize and compensate for the impacts of the proposed activity on the environment and health" as well as other recommendations that emerged from the process of further developing the proposed investment plan (the authorisation procedure under specific regulations).

To verify the expected impacts and determine the true extent of impacts of the proposed building structures on the environment, the assessment report stated a requirement for *monitoring activities* of the relevant phenomena, namely,

- monitoring of visitor numbers;
- monitoring of noise;
- monitoring of emissions;
- monitoring of carnivores;
- monitoring of small terrestrial mammals (Rodentia, Soricimorpha);
- monitoring of birds;
- monitoring of amphibians;
- monitoring of habitats.

The land-use plan for the village of Terchová (Change and amendment no. 2) (Kristiník et al., 2010) assumed the assessed building construction and *supported* it. The territorial plan, as well as other development documents of the village and the region, consider the further development of the site (based on the then upcoming territorial general plan of tourism development), not only in terms of accommodation, but also catering, sports facilities, amenities, services and infrastructure.

In the position of the District Environmental Office on Change and Amendment no. 2 of the territorial plan for Terchová it states: "After negotiation with the Regional Environmental Office, State Nature Protection, Malá Fatra NP, the regional environment office issued an addendum to statement in which it adopted the conclusions that the addressed accommodation capacity is acceptable from the perspective of the ECC of the area of Vrátna Dolina in question ...."

Also on the basis of the above facts we can consider the territory in question in terms of the proposed activity to have sufficient capacity.

3.2.4 Conclusion

This contribution provides an outline of the simple determination of ecological carrying capacity for the needs of the environmental impact assessment. Such a requirement may result from the structure of the compulsory assessment report in accordance with Annex 11 of the EIA Act, from the defined scope of assessment, from the content of relevant strategic documents (particularly land-use planning documentation), etc.

The presented assessment used available sources of information about the area and the available evidence of landscape-ecological and socio-economic nature. For assessment, a greatly simplified modification of the procedure was used to evaluate ECC using the ECC methodology. The evaluation was based on selected properties primary, secondary and tertiary landscape structure. Comprehensiveness required evaluating other features too, e.g. the vulnerability of groundwater and surface water, the vulnerability of air, plants, animals, habitats, as well as factors of well-being and quality of life of man. We believe that for the needs of this particular assessment of the environmental impact, such an approach can be regarded as sufficient.

In conclusion it should be noted that the scale of grading assessed phenomenon or properties is schematic and leads to generalisations and loss of individuality and specificity. Finally, it is necessary to take into account that the outcomes of similar evaluations are always marked by a high degree of subjectivity of the evaluator.

Notwithstanding the above, we consider the presented procedure as superior for determining the carrying capacity of the landscape as generally usable as either part of the landscape-ecological assessment in the development of planning, strategic environmental assessment and when assessing each proposed activity on the environment. From that it then depends on the selection of specific data and details of the evaluation criteria. In the impact assessment process for the proposed activities on the environment it is necessary to take account of the location, nature and extent of the proposed activities and the characteristics and condition of the affected area.

3.3 Agriculture and rural development plan of the Slovak Republic over the 2000–2006 period

3.3.1 Background and purpose of the environmental appraisal

Policies of European Union require the integration of environmental concerns into EU programmes and policies. Agriculture and rural development is one of the key sectors where such an integration is a priority.

The pre-accession strategy of the EC was further intensified with the adoption of the so-called Agenda 2000 in 1997. Two new instruments were to be introduced for the period 2000–2006 in order to prepare candidate countries for EU membership. The first one was ISPA, aimed on interventions and improvements in the environmental and transport structures, the second was SAPARD. This instrument has been introduced to support candidate countries in the activities of adapting their agricultural sector together with rural development and in adoption of the *environmental acquis and sustainable development as a concept.*

Rural development plans under SAPARD should attempt to complement local and regional land-use and development plans. The focus of SAPARD on improving the competitiveness of rural areas should also be balanced with the objective of maintaining the natural and cultural heritage of rural areas. Spatial planning can be used to ensure balanced and sustainable development within rural areas.

The SAPARD Regulation (EC) No. 1268/1999 includes the requirement for ex ante evaluation/prior appraisal. The appraisal is imposed by Articles 3(1), 4(2) and 5 (1) of the above-mentioned SAPARD Regulation. In addition, the implementing Regulation No. 2759/1999 specifies that appraisals shall be carried out taking into account the evaluation requirements provided in Title IV Chapter III of Regulation (EC) No. 1260/99 and Section 5 of Regulation No. 1750/1999.

3.3.2 Scope of the prior appraisal and its implementation

According to the guideline document entitled "SAPARD, Prior Appraisal of Programme Proposals" and "Working Document on Common Indicators for Monitoring of Rural Development Programming" there are the following key issues:

- an assessment of the quantified description of the current situation concerning the disparities, shortcomings and potential for development;
- an assessment of the main results of previous operations undertaken with Community assistance, the financial resources deployed and the evaluation results available;
- the environmental assessment of the strategy proposed by its quantified objectives, the priorities selected and the geographical scope;
- an analysis of the anticipated environmental impact;
- an assessment of the implementing provisions including those for monitoring and evaluation and proposed quantified indicators for evaluation.

3.3.3 Methodology

The environmental appraisal methodology has taken into account the main philosophy of EU Strategic Environmental Assessment Handbooks

(Guidance on Environmental Appraisal: Towards sustainable rural development in the context of SAPARD, DLG, 1999, A Handbook on environmental assessment of regional development plans and EU Structural Funds programmes, EC, DGXI) with four key steps:

1. the environmental baseline;
2. scoping objectives and priorities;
3. environmental appraisal of the draft plan;
4. implementation issues and integrating findings.

Furthermore, the evaluation has taken into account aspects such as rationale, relevance, coherence, potential for effectiveness and efficiency. The appraisal has made a check for the degree to which the *assistance is transformed into intermediate and global impacts such as improved rural conditions and protection of rural environment.*

3.3.4 Analysis of the current situation

3.3.4.1 Analysis of the environmental situation of the region/sector concerned, the main strength and disparities/shortcomings, the opportunities for and threats to rural development (SWOT analysis) and potential for development

With regard to both agriculture and rural areas, there is an *interdependence* between those activities and the quality of environment. At the same time the agriculture directly depends on the environmental quality. Agriculture participates on polluting the environment by its economic activities and on decreasing its ecological stability. But on the other hand, agriculture and rural development play a positive role in forming the rural landscape (so-called landscape administration), its diversity and species diversity. Under SAPARD Plan evaluators can understand the Plan for both agricultural sector and *rural landscape development*. It means it is not predominantly the issue of the sector of agriculture since it has a great possibility to help improving environmental conditions of the country.

At present, the state system in Slovakia is subject to the transition processes from centrally planned economy towards market oriented economy. This process includes comprehensive restructuring activities in economy, legislation, state administration as well as the financial and social sectors. Similarly, parallel changes in agriculture and environmental spheres are take place in this process.

As far as the natural conditions are considered the environmental aspects are of high importance in agriculture and rural development. Slovakia is a variegated country with a range of landscape types due to the fact that geomorphologically the territory is a part of the Carpathian mountains range and lowlands are the part of Panonia basin. Such variety of natural components, and the geological conditions in particular, influence the spatial distribution of soil categories and types which in turn determines the status and the structure of biodiversity as well as fertility. All forms of contamination, degradation or modification of environmental components (air, water, soil) directly or indirectly lead to a reduction of biodiversity.

The agricultural land represents 49.9 % of the total Slovak area. Due to non-systematic and non-environmentally - friendly steps oriented towards intensive utilisation of natural resources, many plants as well as animal species are extinct, and many are threatened. Furthermore, the population is concentrated in lowlands and valleys, the mountain areas show but low population densities, and, as a result, extensive settlements and land utilisation had a material impact on the original landscape structure as well as on ecosystems.

There are about 1210 villages with less than 500 inhabitants and 95.8% Slovak settlements are considered to be rural settlements. They take 59,5% of the total area with 62.8% of agricultural land and 55.9% forests in it. The settlement and spatial aspects in rural development are significant since they are derived from the geomorphologic, socio-economic and environmental/sustainability conditions. This was not in the practice up to now.

The analysis of the current environmental situation in Slovakia brings summary of relevant environmental baseline for inclusion in draft Plan, highlighting the key pressures and areas of importance and the links with environmental policy and legislation and the assessment of the links between environmental issues and key driving forces (land-use and economic activities).

Identification of the data gaps have taken place in the analysis.

The following presents all steps of the analysis:

- list of relevant environmental aspects - state of the environment data together with economic and social baseline data;
- environmental problems and opportunities and key issues, (areas subject to continuing environmental deterioration, areas of particular importance and value);
- zoning areas;
- environmental policy and legislation;
- links with land-use/agricultural activities;
- relevant policy objectives and legislation at the international, EU, na-

tional and regional level (Ramsar, Bern Conventions, Birds and Habitats Directive);
- assessing the baseline information (SWOT analysis, links with economic activities, the main pressures on the environment from economic sector, activities and types of development);
- explanation of environmental baseline relevance to the Plan and the types of measures which can be funded under SAPARD.

The territory of Slovakia belongs to the most polluted ones in Europe. Water and air especially show pollution above average. In terms of environmental regionalisation, 37.5% of Slovak people live on 10% of the territory with disturbed and strongly disturbed environment.

Over the past decade, positive changes have taken place in Slovakia in the quality of some environmental components, however, substantial improvement did not occur. There was a reduction in the amount of emissions released into air, and also in the amount of waters polluted by sewage. This reduction can be assigned not only to increased protection measures, but largely to phasing out of economic activities.

The consequences of the disturbed ecological stability of the country are demonstrated more and more profoundly in direct and indirect economic and social loses, with visible impacts on businesses and the state budget. A large part of Slovak territory, especially in agricultural areas, is ecologically unstable.

The next part brings the summary of *relevant environmental aspects* in relation to the agricultural activities/practices and to the rural development of the area covered by SAPARD Plan. These are likely to be important (see Tab. 14). This is just a summary. The detailed quantification aspects can be found in the SAPARD Plan of the Slovak Republic.

Tab. 14: Environmental aspects for the baseline

Water: • quality of surface and ground waters including drinking water, covering pollution aspects related to nutrients, organic substances, chemicals (nitrates, pesticides, leakage from silage juices, eutrofication) • quantity of surface water and groundwater including catchment management aspects (irrigation, dewatering)
Soil: • soil quality (physical degradation of soil, compacting of soils, acidification, fertility, heavy metals, salinity, humus content, contamination, biological degradation, sludge from waste water treatment plant) • soil erosion and compaction
Air: • emissions of greenhouse gases (CO2, NOxCH4, N2O, NH3, VOC)

Natural resources and landscape protection: • protected areas • other areas and sites of high natural value (Emerald network) • endangered ecosystems and species (biodiversity of the flora and the zoocenoses within the agricultural landscape, irrigation, dewatering, melioration/land improvement) • landscape and countryside values, including cultural heritage
Human resources: • health conditions • living aspects (agriculture as the main economic activity is decreasing, landscape administration, tourism, entrepreneurial activities for processing products)
Risk factors • waste (sludge waste water)
Institutional aspects • relationship among organisational, technical and technological procedures of agriculture to environmental stability, biodiversity and environmental conditions within the agricultural landscape) • monitoring (the entire area monitoring, regional monitoring, local or special purpose monitoring)

Source: Belčáková (2000)

Territorial, regional development as well as rural development of Slovakia shall be directed towards the achievement of territorial-wide system of ecological stability, genetic resources and biodiversity conservation, saving cultural heritage and also towards optimal land use.

It is necessary to strengthen the ecological stability of the country primarily in the areas where ecologically stabile element are absent, i.e. in the antropogentically heavily modified country.

Furthermore, another zoning areas aspect is a 3-grade spatial division of the country based on the ratio between eco-stabilisation elements and stress inducing factors, e.g. between potential and limits.

SAPARD Plan comprises several measures affecting particular types of habitats or geographical areas. That is why "landscape approach" should be taken by identifying zones within the geographical area of SAPARD Plan and types of agricultural landscape and their uses in respect to natural and landscape protection. *Since this spatial dimension is not employed in the SAPARD Plan the evaluators would like to stress this fact.* This is important for more targeted measures. The most affected and degraded areas include lowland, meadows and wetland ecosystems.

In the past as well as over the last decade (by 1997) there was no coherent agrarian and rural development policy. Environmental activities and measures were just partial ones. Unfortunately, there was *no effective co-operation* and integrated action neither at national nor at regional levels.

Evaluators have considered the environmental policy and legislation *relevant* to the objectives of the SAPARD Plan and the measures proposed to implement it. The following important national and EU legislation and policies are highlighted (Annex 1)

Further details on EU policies and legislation procedures can be found in Annex VI of the SAPARD Plan (Acqui implementation in environmental legislation).

Based on the SWOT analysis of the Slovak SAPARD Plan as well as on the actual assessment of the situation in the country the following list of main *weaknesses and threats* can be observed:

Weaknesses of the natural environment in Slovakia

- *pollution and degradation of the environmental media (air, water, soil, biodiversity) as a result of agricultural practices;*
- *high rates of soil erosion (caused by water in mountains and by wind in lowland areas);*
- *high ploughing rates of agricultural land;*
- *damage caused to forests by immissions and pests;*
- *low number of communities connected to technical infrastructure (sewage system, water pipeline, etc.);*
- *lack of public information about sustainability issues related to the country;*
- *disrupted ecological stability of parts of the country with negative impacts on sustainable rural development;*
- *growing problems with the maintenance of a cultural landscape due to collapsing agriculture;*
- *low level of waste recycling and utilisation, as well as of utilisation of renewable energy sources.*

Threats of the natural environment in Slovakia

- *threat to environmental quality by cumulation of pollution;*
- *exhaustion of natural resources;*
- *pollution impacts on human health;*
- *expected growth of industrial production volumes;*
- *lack of investment in order to maintain the environmental monitoring system;*
- *growing car traffic;*
- *low level of environmental awareness;*

- *a lack of intersectoral co-operation in order to meet sustainability requirements.*

Apart from weaknesses and threats, opportunities and strengths for the sustainable agriculture and rural development were analysed:

Strengths of natural environment in Slovakia

- *high standard of environmental protection;*
- *existence of valuable parts of the country in good shapes (3 locations are on the List of World Cultural Heritage, 12 locations are included in the List of World Natural Heritage, and other localities are in the selection process for nomination to both lists);*
- *great potential for recreation and leisure time activities;*
- *diversity of the rural area and developed communities on it;*
- *environmental regionalisation implemented;*
- *periodic monitoring and assessment of environmental quality,*
- *high degree of biodiversity preservation, in particular in mountain regions;*
- *slovakia´s participation and involvement in many international environmental conferences and conventions;*
- *high proportions of protected areas aimed at natural protection,*
- *extensive areas covered by forests;*
- *balanced ratio of agricultural to forest land areas;*
- *variegated nature of the landscape and sufficient landscape potential;*
- *significant hydrologic potential of surface and ground waters;*
- *Reduction of environmental pollution degree during recent years (in particular concerning air);*
- *presence of professional and well-managed programmes for environmental protection.*

Identification of needs resulting from the analysis of weaknesses and opportunities

- *with regard to the above-mentioned SWOT analysis there can be recognised several major relevant environmental needs in the development of agriculture and rural areas:*
- *more employment opportunities in the so-called land administration;*
- *technical infrastructure development in rural areas;*
- *territorial planning documentation development in rural areas;*
- *correct, environmental friendly farming on soil;*
- *to establish irrigation principles that consider environmental aspects,* e.g. (modification of soils water regime by irrigation to manage in order

to fulfil requirements of environment, *positive ecological impacts – by finishing of construction of drinking and utility water supplies for farms, to increase biodiversity and stability of agricultural landscape by expanding cultivation methods favourable utilising natural sources of the landscape, by regulation and management of water in agricultural landscape to integrate waters to the hydrological and biological production cycle in agri-ecosystem by effective utilisation of water as a non-alternative production factor to optimise application of synthetic fertilisers and pesticides from the point of view of environmental protection,to extend ecological management on the basis of sources like water, soil, sunshine);*
- *agricultural production methods focusing on the protection of the environment and the landscape are being supported and implemented in Slovakia;*
- *to develop ecological agriculture processes (transformation of arable land to pastures – grassing, keeping of local breeds of animals, development of agri-environmental schemes);*
- *production of good quality food in a more extensive and environmentally more friendly way;*
- *projects of land consolidation based on territorial systems of ecological stability;*
- *environmentally firendly forest management;*
- *higher environmental awareness;*
- *better intersectoral co-operation.*

The above-mentioned trends in the state of the environment are being affected mainly by the following agricultural activities:
- large-scale breeding of cattle and swine;
- Plant production;
- conversion of meadows and forest areas into arable soil;
- animal production – livestock breeding, mainly its intensive form;
- application of chemical preparations for plant treatment;
- mineral fertilisers application;
- pesticides application;
- nutrient discharge;
- dewatering and irrigation;
- melioration/land improvement;
- soil compaction;
- utilisation of heavy machinery and incorrect farming on soils (structure of plant production, seeding procedures, fertilisation);
- incorrect swapping of crops;
- land-use intensity;

3.3.5 Analysis of previous operations

National Development Strategy which forms a part of the Integrated Regional and Social Development Plan of the Slovak Republic for Phare 2000 implementation covers the issue of rural and agricultural development. It is in *compliance* with the Accession Partnership priorities as well as the National Programme for the Adoption of the Acquis Communautaire. The SAPARD Plan has been elaborated in accordance with priorities of the *Integrated Regional and Social Plan* of the SR as well as the provisions of EC Regulations No. 1268/1999 (Articles 3 (1), 4(2), 5(1)) and 2759/1999.

There have been several programmes towards rural development in relation to EU standards under *Phare* and special programmes under SPP.

Preparatory Committee for structural funds has been set up in the Slovak Republic with the task to co-ordinate the SPP, SAPARD, Phare 2000+ and environmental ISPA programmes.

In Slovakia, there have been two programmes that should have a *real environmental compliance with Slovak SAPARD Plan, namely with measure No.6 and No. 7. – "Agri- environmental programme" and "Natura 2000 - Pilot Project on Emerald network in Slovakia".*

The first one was financed by Dutch Ministry of Agriculture, Nature and Fisheries Management. The Task Force was established in Slovakia for the implementation of the Agri/environmental Programme (IUCN Slovakia) who, later, developed analysis of the environmental conditions of agriculture in Slovakia.

As a result the pilot area was selected for the implementation of the agri-environmental program (being the biospheric reserve Poľana).

The "Agri-environmental Program for Slovakia" is being developed (expected to be completed by the end of the 1st half-year of 2000), along with the Draft Pilot Agri-environmental Program for the Selected Area of Poľana. The second one has been based on the support of Council of Europe and European Commission.

Cooperation and coordination of the Council of Europe (responsible for the Bern Convention) with the European Commission (responsible for the Habitats and Birds Directives) are beneficial both from the professional and financial point of view and they break historic, political and economic barriers in nature protection. This procedure helps the candidate countries for EU accession in their preparation for implementation of the Habitats Directive, because the procedure for predetermination of ASCI from the formal aspect is fully compatible with the first phase of building the NATURA 2000 network; if these countries establish a coherent ASCI network within the Emerald network, they will have an advantage in creating the national list of sites and their application into NATURA 2000.

Implementation phase for Emerald network started in 1999. Years 1999 - 2000 represent the initial phase, in which most of the countries involved in this process will start with implementation of pilot projects, supported by the Council of Europe. In 1999 the implementation of this project started also in Slovakia.

Area of protected areas of nature and landscape currently covers 22.8 % of the territory of SR; there is a presumption that up to 25% of the territory of SR will be included into the Emerald network.

Evaluators would like to stress that several environmental programmes/ activities have been launched under Phare, Phare CBC, Phare DISAE and ISPA. A lot of them have relation to agriculture and rural development. These ones should be added to the draft Plan in order to be clear about the compatibility with them.

3.3.6 Assessment of the relevance and consistency of the proposed strategy

3.3.6.1 Justification and relevance of the strategy and its priorities for actions

This section is based on the analysis of relation between key issues in the SAPARD Plan to the current environmental situation and the overall objectives that have derived from it.

Another focus on analysis has been put on the appropriate sectors, geographical areas, populations/beneficiaries addressed in the SAPARD Plan (Belčáková, 2000).

Enclosures 6 and 7 brings the overall summary of the whole SAPARD Plan indicating its overall development framework, main targets, strategic targets and operational objectives.

As a first step the assessment of the relevance between the objectives of SAPARD Plan and needs for the development of agricultural sector and rural areas has been conducted. The major needs have resulted from the SWOT analysis presented in previous part. The assessment has been mainly performed at the general objective level. Then the assessment of relevance between strategic and specific goals has taken place in order to get clear to what degree the strategic and specific goals (objectives) meet those needs.

As a last step, we have been looking at operational objectives.

The main outputs from this assessment are:

a) Rural development objectives and agriculture primary sector objectives incorporate environmental sustainability considerations, e.g. use of renewable resources within limits of capacity for generation, environmentally sound use and management of hazardous/polluting substances, conservation and enhancement the status of wildlife, habitats and landscapes, maintenance and improvement the quality of soils and water resources, maintenance and improvement of local environmental quality, protection of atmosphere, development of environmental awareness, education and training, promotion of public participation in decisions involving sustainable development.
b) There is a high relevance between strategic goals, specific and operational objectives and environmental needs addressing both European and national levels.

Based on the assessment it can be conclude that majority of actual environmental needs that are relevant for agriculture primary sector and rural development are covered either by strategic goals or specific and operational objectives.

Concerning the appropriate sectors, geographical areas and populations/beneficiaries addressed there is a high relevance between environmental needs and objectives under priority 2, measure No. 6 "Environmentally friendly agricultural methods". It has to be said that it is not very clear whether environmental aspect has been considered for geographical areas under Priority No. 1 – all measures. Priority No. 3 has more or less horizontal geographical aspect.

3.3.6.2 Consistency between operational and global objectives (internal environmental coherence)

The appropriate hierarchy of objectives has been assessed. The actual environmental assessment has been conducted at two levels:

a) the general objectives and the specific objectives of SAPARD Plan;
b) the specific objectives and the measures of SAPARD Plan.

The Annex 2 and 3 represent the outcomes of expert judgement on the above-mentioned issues.

From the above table it is evident that priorities of SAPARD Plan and appropriate measures are drafted in a cohesive and coordinated way as far as concerns the environmental factors.

There is also coherence between SAPARD Plan operational objectives and general eligibility criteria (...beneficiary shall comply with EU and the

Slovak national environmental standards screening for environmental impact....)

3.3.6.3 Balance between the different support measures of the plan

Since agriculture and especially rural development measures have environmental/intersectoral aspect the Rural Development Policy needs to be elaborated and implemented in accordance with the close cooperation among different ministries/programmes/groups in order to ensure the coherence and integrated way of their realisation.

SAPARD Plan in its draft mentions the need for such co-operation under the title 1.8. Environment. What is missing is the information on detailed co-operation strategies with Ministry for the Environment and other Ministries that are inter-linked with environmental and sustainability issues not only in the step of drafting the SAPARD Plan but in its implementation as well (e.g. what is the direct involvement of Ministry for the Environment and Slovak Environmental Agency in the implementation of SAPARD Plan?)

3.3.6.4 Adequacy between the proposed plan and other relevant policies and programmes (external environmental coherence)

The external coherence of environmental objectives and priorities for Rural development for the programming period of 2000–2006 between SAPARD Plan and other relevant programmes and policies has been also evaluated.

As far as Common Agricultural Policy (CAP)concerns the objective No. 5 puts an emphasis on "an agricultural sector that is sustainable in environmental terms, contributes to the preservation of natural resources and the natural heritage and maintains the visual amenity of the countryside". Since the Slovak SAPARD Plan is focused on the development of a sustainable and competitive agriculture within the overall economic development of rural country we can say that there is such external coherence.

The basic general environmental objectives of the SAPARD Plan (in relation to " Policy paper for rural development of the Slovak Republic") are the need to preserve the ecological approach and sustainable development of rural areas as well as the quality of life of rural population.

Priorities of SAPARD Plan (1. Improvement of agricultural production sector including the food industry, 2. Sustainable rural development, 3. Development of human resources) follow the objectives below:

a) to help in making the agricultural primary production more effective with an emphasis on animal welfare and environment (Priority No.1);

b) to help ensuring appropriate living standard and improvement of life quality of rural inhabitants, creation of convenient social conditions (Priority No.2);
c) to help with conservation of cultural heritage values of the rural areas and the countryside. (Priority No.2)
d) to help to harmonise the environmental aspect of SAPARD Plan in the framework of territorial planning at national, regional and local levels.

Agrarian and Food Industry Policy declared the midterm objective focusing on strengthening the efficiency and competitiveness of the agri-food sector to adequately utilise domestic production factors in order to participate in international trade with respect to the environmental and social functions of agriculture. One if its pilot schemes are environmental measures with agro-environmental programme and environmental investments.

Environmental programme objectives of Slovak Forest Policy are aimed at the mitigation of impacts on forests resulting from antropogenic harmful agents, from both domestic and out country immissions on forests. Similarly one of its programmes consider the monitoring of forest status including the protection, as well as revitalisation measures in damaged forests.

Measures No. 8 and 9 have a lot of common features with the Village Renovation Programme for Slovakia the main objective of which is diversification of rural activities, revitalisation of villages, technical infrastructure development as well as to ensure the landscape protection in Slovak villages.

The draft SAPARD Plan does not present the link to the appropriate State Environmental Policy or to the National Environmental Action Plan.We find it very important to be completed since the Rural Development Plan is not only the agricultural plan but the environmental one as well. This interrelation in the strategic part discussing on objectives and priorities is absolutely missing.

3.3.7 Assessment of the expected impacts of the selected priorities

3.3.7.1 Identification and evaluation of the expected environmental impacts of the selected impacts and results that would follow-on from the measures of the plan

The expected impacts of selected priorities and measures are presented in the form of environmental appraisal matrices of the draft Plan and options considered. They are accompanied by a short written commentary on key issues raised.

The following steps has been undertaken:

- draft Plan and options – types of measures, location of measures
- matrices
- appraisal factors, significance, uncertainty, cumulative effects

3.3.7.2 Environmental indicators for future monitoring

The Annex 4 below shows the summary of some of expected environmental indicators for future monitoring based on the evaluation matrices and expert judgement. Some of them occurred in the text of SAPARD Plan. Evaluators would like the SAPARD Task Force to add them into the text. OECD indicators of sustainable agriculture should also be utilised in determining evaluation and monitoring indicators in draft Plan.

3.3.8 Verification of the proposed implementing arrangements

3.3.8.1 Clear definition of responsibilities

The SAPARD Plan has clearly described the administrative framework at national (National Steering Committee and National Monitoring Committee, SAPARD Agency) and regional level (regional Offices of the Ministry of Agriculture of the Slovak Republic, Regional Secretariats at NUTS III level, Regional Steering Committees for SAPARD). Furthermore, general indicative plan of financing, financing plan according to individual years and measures, institutions granting financial means and rules for funds allocation are provided.

Unfortunately, one can not get clear about the practical involvement of environmental entities (Ministry of Environment, Slovak Environmental Agency, etc....) in the implementation process of SAPARD Plan. There was a certain cooperation between Ministry of Environment and Ministry of Agriculture in the preparation of SAPARD Plan. It should be stressed that the involvement of NGO in National Steering Committee and National Monitoring Committee for SAPARD is a positive feature.

3.3.8.2 Arrangements for the correct implementation of the programme, in particular for monitoring and evaluation

As to the monitoring and evaluation arrangements the mechanism for modification of the programme, reports and evaluation in particular periods of time, the ways of inspection and sanction measures as well as informing and publicity arrangements are described in the draft of SAPARD Plan. Similarly, it seems that no environmental entity will take part in the monitoring and evaluation processes.

3.3.8.3 Procedures and selection criteria defined in order to reinforce the project selection in terms of effectiveness and efficiency

Selection and eligibility criteria are well described within the different measures of the SAPARD Plan. They are in compliance with EU environmental standards and, also, take into account ecological considerations that are now proposed as general conditions for project approval.

Methodological instructions concerning project submission details are going to be provided by the MoA SR.

3.3.9 Conclusions and recommendations

It should be noted that this is only the environmental part of the ex-ante evaluation of Rural Development Plan of the Slovak Republic.

It has been divided into the following topics which logically follow one by one:

- environmental baseline analysis summarising the environmental data, zoning aspects, current and past policy framework, link to agricultural activities and SWOT analysis, major environmental needs as the most important outcome from this part;
- consistency between the proposed strategy and selected targets with the existing environmental situation in the regions of Slovakia;
- to clarify the environmental objectives of the Plan, their relevance to the needs, expected environmental impacts of the co-financed activities;
- consistency between the different hierarchy of objectives;
- relation to acquis communaitaire concerning important environmental documents and policies, sustainable agriculture;
- definition of quantified environmental indicators for evaluation and monitoring;
- environmental provisions for implementation, monitoring and evaluation.

As a result of the analysis and assessment in each above-mentioned topic, the following recommendations are formulated (Belčáková, 2000):

a) A screening procedure to appraise the likely environmental impact of the project will be undertaken, involving the competent environmental authorities, in all cases where any significant negative impact might reasonably be anticipated. It will decide whether an Environmental Impact Assessment (EIA) must be carried out or not. This screening procedure may be based on a case by case examination or on threshold criteria, which should be made available to the Commission. In any case, the projects listed in Annex 1 of the Directive 97/11 and in Annex 1 of the national Act No. 127/94 will be subject to an EIA.

b) An agreement on the project by the competent environmental authority must be provided for those projects where any significant negative impact on the environment could reasonably be anticipated and in particular for those covered by measures 1, 2, 4, 5, 7. Information should be given on the potential negative effects of the project (e.g. chemical use, emissions, atmospheric, water and soil pollutants) and the method of their attenuation particularly in the environmental sensitive areas.

c) The assessment should be carried out by the authorised expert according to the Decree of the Ministry of Environment SR No.52/1995 Coll. on list of professionally eligible persons to perform environmental impact assessment. The involvement of environmental authorities in drawing up the plan and the extent to which their comments were incorporated – the information is still not provided.

d) To take into account the elaboration of TSES during the creation of land-use/territorial plans, forest management plans, water management plans, re-cultivation plans, project of land consolidation.

e) Several environmental programmes/activities have been launched under Phare, Phare CBC, Phare DISAE and ISPA. A lot of them have relation to agriculture and rural development. These ones should be added to the draft Plan in order to be clear about the compatibility with them.

f) The information on detailed co-operation strategies with Ministry for the Environment and other Ministries that are inter-linked with environmental and sustainability issues not only in the step of drafting the SAPARD Plan but in its implementation as well are missing (e.g. what is the direct involvement of Ministry for the Environment and Slovak Environmental Agency in the implementation and monitoring of SAPARD programmes and projects). These should be included.

g) The link to the appropriate State Environmental Policy or to the National Environmental Action Plan activities towards agriculture and rural development should be completed since the Rural Development Plan is not only the agricultural plan but the environmental one as well. This interrelation in the strategic part discussing on objectives and priorities is absolutely missing.

h) To get clear about the practical involvement of environmental entities (Ministry of Environment, Slovak Environmental Agency, etc....) in the implementation and monitoring processes of the SAPARD Plan that should be very clearly declared in the plan.

3.4 Evaluation of landscape ecological stability in TSES Kocurany

3.4.1 Ecological stability of the system and spatial ecological stability of the landscape

Evaluating the stability of elements of the PLS should express the total value of the various elements for their environment and therefore for the development of environmental systems. This is based on the assumption that the relative degree of ecological stability is inversely proportional to the intensity of anthropic influence on the ecosystem.

Thus, the level of ecological stability of the country depends on the variety and arrangement of its elements and the strength of its internal links. The higher intrinsic environmental quality an element of the present landscape structure (PLS) has based on its biological, ecological, as well as other utilitarian functions, the higher is its ecological quality, and the larger is its positive influence on the area, e.g. having higher water-retention, anti-erosion, filter capacity, higher protective, hygienic, aesthetic functions. Of course on the other hand, the degree of quality of elements of PLS is also influenced by the negative phenomena that can greatly affect the quality of the elements. One of the criteria is a comparison of the potential and current state of ecosystems in the landscape.

For assessing the significance of landscape elements for ecological stability a 5-point scale is often used as per Löw et al. (1995):

1. without importance (e.g. built-upon areas and roads with asphalt or concrete surface);
2. minor importance (e.g. large-block fields, intensive vineyards, hop-growing, etc.);
3. medium importance (in terms of the objectives of TSES this is attributed to intensified meadows, extensive use of permanent crops, etc.);
4. high importance (e.g. extensively used grassland, mixed forests, etc.);
5. very high importance (especially indigenous and natural forests, natural herbaceous communities, wetlands, peat bogs, rivers and areas with

natural bottom and sides characteristic of the aquatic and riparian communities).

By processing the classification of the ecological quality of each component of the area's PLS, we get important information for identifying ecologically important segments of the landscape.

For evaluating the ecological stability of the country, for the area of interest – the area of land modification in Kocurany cadastral area the following formula is used to calculate the coefficient of ecological stability (quality) of the territory (Miklós 1986, Jurko, 1990):

$$K_{ES} = \sum_{1}^{n} \frac{p_i . S_{SKŠi}}{p}$$

where:

K_{ES} coefficient of ecological stability of the area of interest

p_i total area of individual types of elements of landscape structure (ha)

S_{SKSi} degree of ecological quality of the i-th element of PLS

p total area of the area of interest (ha)

n number of elements of landscape structure in the area of interest

Areas of individual mapped elements of the PLS of the area of interest, their degree of ecological quality (S_{SKSi}) as well as the coefficient of ecological stability of the territory (K_{ES}) are presented in Tab. 15 and in Fig. 27.

Tab. 15: Areas of individual elements of PLS in the Kocurany area of land modification and the relevant values of K_{ES}

Elements of PLS	**Area (ha)**	**S_{SKSi}**	**K_{ES}**
Forests	101.36	4	1.22
Groups of NFWV of an indigenous character	25.54	4	0.31
Riparian growth	8.04	4	0.09
Line NFWV of an indigenous character	2.36	3	0.02
Vegetation of waterlogged meadows with Phragmites communis	0.06	4	0.00
Extensively exploited meadows and pasture	39.54	3	0.36
Intensively exploited meadows and pasture	84.11	2	0.51
Large-block arable land	59.59	1	0.18
Small-block arable land	0.85	2	0.00
Gardens	0.14	2	0.00
Mosaic structures	6.67	4	0.08
III. class road and paved field and forest roads	0.35	1	0.00

Non-paved field and forest roads	2.7	2	0.02
Horse-farming grounds and buildings outside the settlement	0.9	1	0.00
Old cemetery	0.27	3	0.00
Total area	332.48		2.79

Source: Diviaková, Kočický et al., 2012 in Diviaková, Kočický, Novikmec, Svitok, 2012

Based on the above, the value of K_{ES}, was calculated, which for the territory represented by the Kocurany land modification area was a value of 2.79 which means that it is landscape with medium ecological stability (see Tab.16). This is due to the fact that the dominant element of the landscape structure is now meadows and pastures which have a low to medium importance for ecological stability (S_{SKSi} = 2-3). The second most abundant element is forests that still represent the most stable element of the monitored area, but their ecological quality is somewhat influenced by imission impairment (S_{SKSi} = 4). The high degree of ecological stability was also assigned to the group of NFWV of an indigenous character, riparian vegetation and mosaic structure meeting many important functions for the landscape. Other elements of PLS (arable land, roads, built-up areas) represent elements of little to no significance.

Tab. 16: Interpretation of K_{ES}

Assessment of landscape	Coefficient of ES	Degree of ES	Ecological measures
Landscape with very low ecological stability	1.00 – 1.49	1	high need to implement new eco-stabilising elements and eco-stabilising management measures
Landscape with low ecological stability	1.5–2.49	2	need to implement new eco-stabilising elements and eco-stabilising management measures
Landscape with medium ecological stability	2.5–3.49	3	conditional necessity to implement new eco-stabilising elements, or application of appropriate management measures
Landscape with high ecological stability	3.5–4.49	4	implementation of appropriate management measures
Landscape with very high ecological stability	4.5–5.00	5	implementation of maintenance management

Source: Pauditšová, Reháčková, Ružičková (2007)

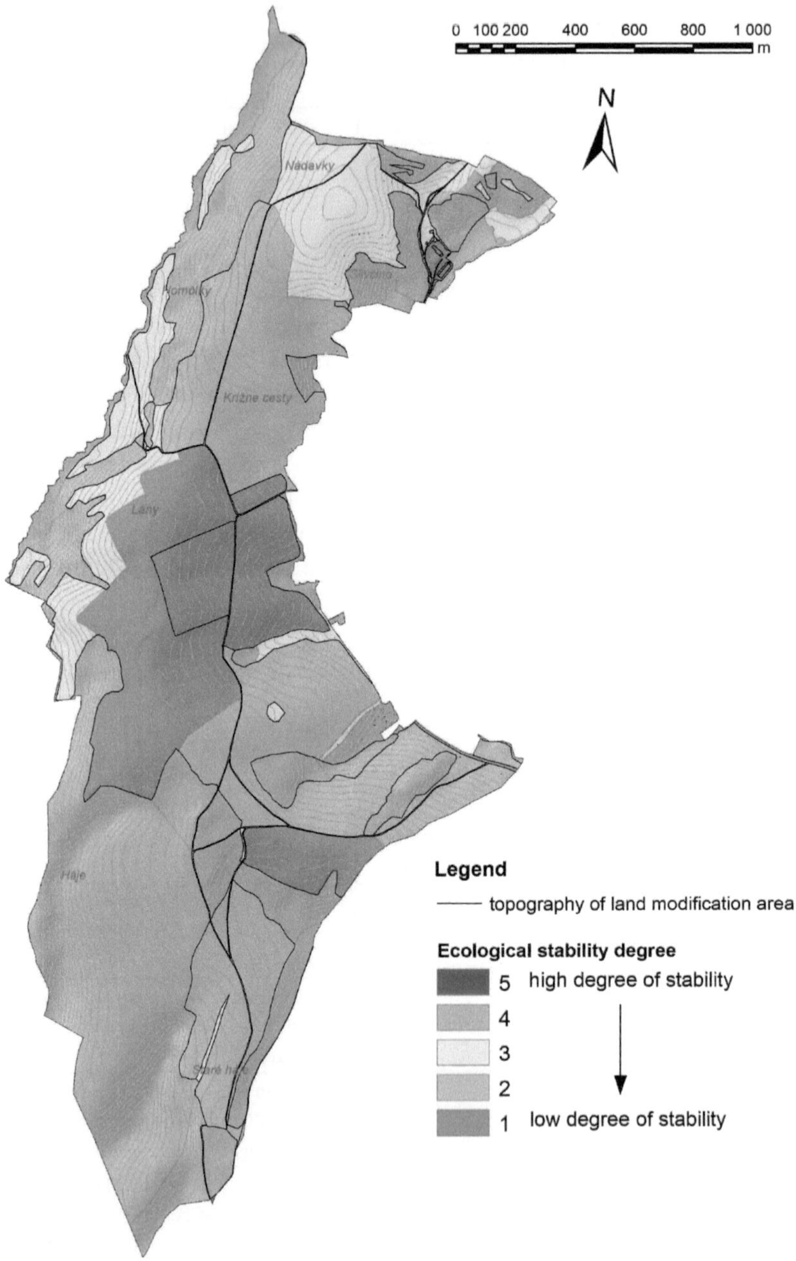

Fig. 27: Spatial ecological stability of the territory based on the degree of ecological stability of CLS elements in the Kocurany land modification area (Diviaková, Kočický, 2012 in Diviaková, Kočický, Novikmec, Svitok, 2012)

From the resulting value of K_{ES} for the Kocurany land modification area it follows that the area requires implementation of measures from the local TSES (appropriate management measures and proposal of new eco-stabilizing elements) to improve the ecological stability of the area.

The criterion of ecological stability forms the basis for marking ecologically important segments of the country (see Tab. 17) Ecologically significant landscape segments (ESLS) are parts of the country, which consist of ecosystems with relatively higher ecological stability or where such ecosystems predominate. They are characterised by the permanence of the biota and ecological conditions, allowing the existence of a kind of natural gene pool of the landscape. In integrating the landscape segments into the skeleton of ecological stability the principle of relative choice is applied. Selected segments are incorporated with the relatively highest value for biodiversity conservation, hence the highest relative internal ecological stability. In general, the skeleton of ecological stability mainly consists of areas classified with the three highest levels of ecological stability (5-3) (Miklós et al., 2011).

In defining the ecological stability of ESLS can be subdivided on the basis of spatial-structural criteria (size and shape, the current state of biota, etc...). A system of such criteria was proposed in the work of e.g. Buček and Lacina (1995); Löw et al. (1995) and Miklós (1996) with the following characteristics (see Fig. 28-30):

- Ecologically important landscape elements – small areas (1-10 hectares) with homogeneous ecological conditions, e.g. a group of trees, a solitaire in agricultural land, natural meadow in the middle of intensively used, fertilizing and ploughed meadows.
- Ecologically significant landscape units – more extensive areas (10 to 1,000 hectares), where there is a variety of environmental conditions allowing the existence of several types of communities, e.g. the upper and middle valleys of rivers with forest, rock and wetland communities. Within the total it is possible to define various important landscape elements.
- Ecologically important areas of large size (generally more than 1000 ha) with diverse ecological conditions and communities with a high proportion of natural communities. These include conservation areas, as well as other large areas with a predominance of natural forests with indigenous tree species composition and species-rich meadow communities. As part of ecologically important landscapes it is appropriate to define important landscape elements, if necessary units and line communities.
- Ecologically significant line communities have an elongated shape and are characterised by a predominance of transient peripheral biota

(Ecotones). The densest network of line communities in the cultural landscape consists of watercourses with riparian vegetation. The major line communities also include avenues and lines of native trees.
- Territorial system of stress factors containing sources of stress factors and areas affected by stress factors, cores and barriers

Tab. 17: Ecologically significant segments in Kocurany area of land modification

ES landscape segment	ID	Characteristics	Degree of ecological stability
Ecol. significant landscape unit (10–1000 ha)	3	Háje a Staré Háje – forest growth	4
	2	Nádavky – forest growth	4
Ecologically significant landscape element (1–10 ha)	6	forest growth	4
	7	forest growth + groups of NFWV of indigenous character	4
	8	forest growth + groups of NFWV of indigenous character	4
	9	forest growth	4
	13	Mosaic of meadows and NFWV (with a share of NFWV over 25 %)	4
Ecologically significant line communities	1	Šútov stream – foothill stream with a continuous riparian vegetation	4
	4	Homôlky – non-forest woody vegetation	4
	5	Jeleškový stream – foothill stream with a riparian vegetation	4
	10	Line NFWV of an indigenous character	3

Source: Diviaková, Kočický et al., 2012; in Diviaková, Kočický, Novikmec, Svitok, 2012)

Preservation of the skeleton of ecological stability is vital for the landscape and the TSES must first use these existing values, as newly proposed elements that need to be created in the country to create, start to perform their functions after several years or several decades (Löw et al. 1995).

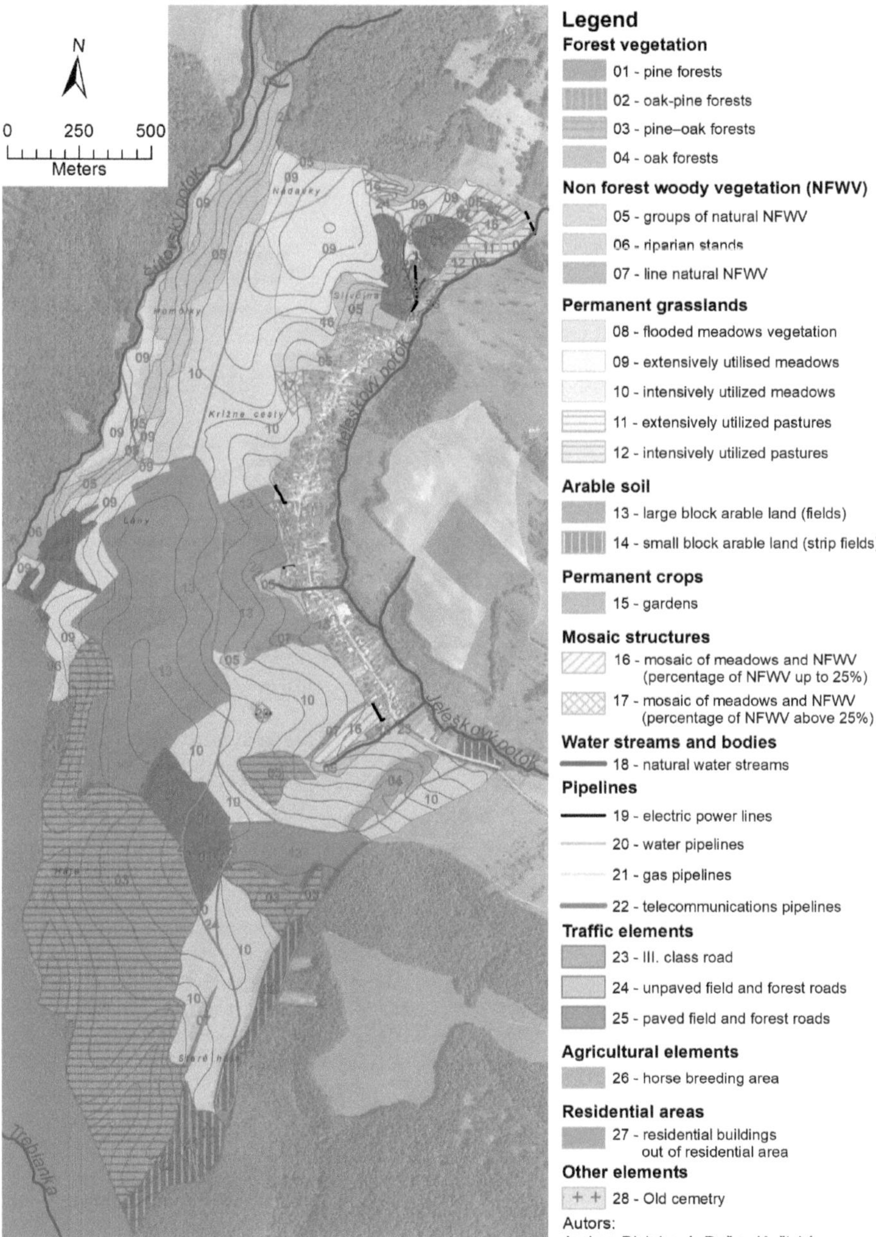

Fig. 28: The present landscape structure (Diviaková, Kočický, 2012 in Diviaková, Kočický, Novikmec, Svitok, 2012)

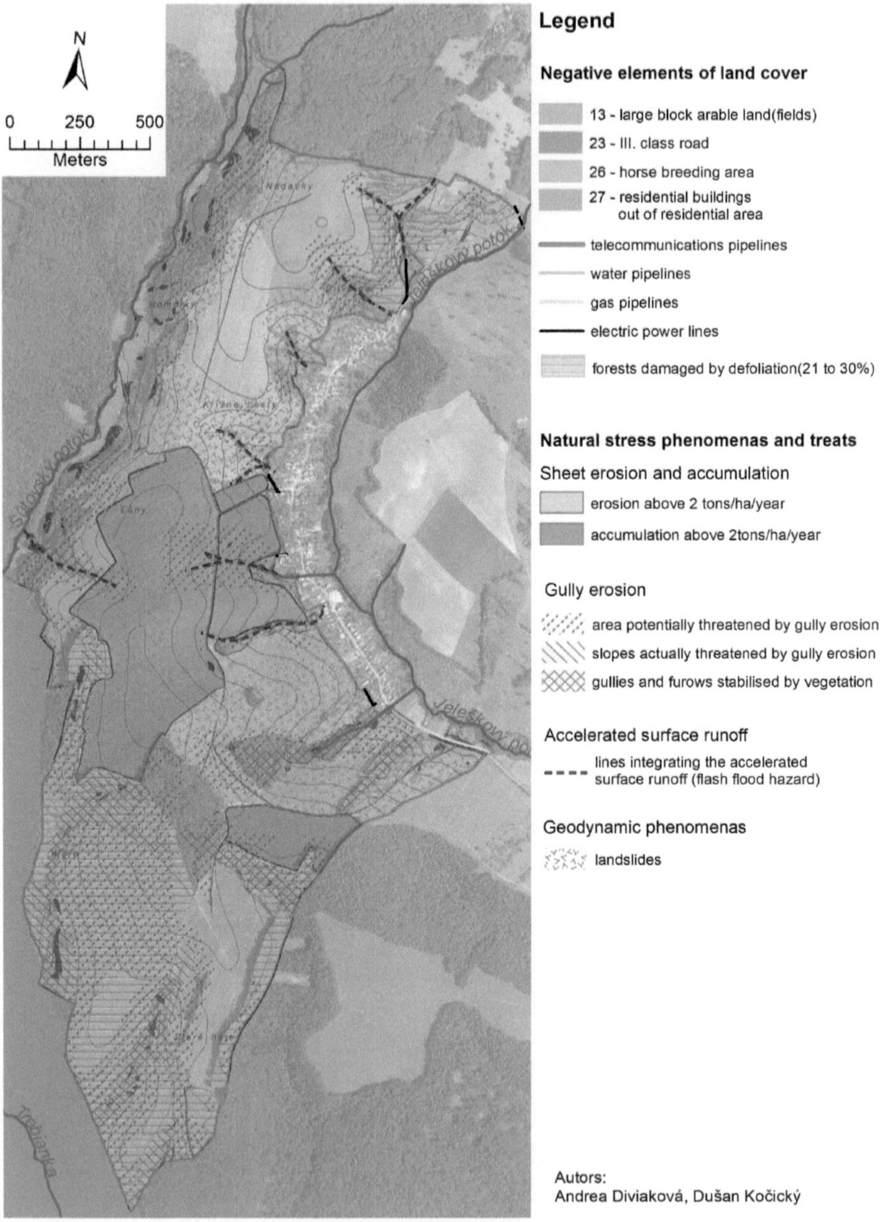

Fig. 29: Territorial system of stress factors (Diviaková, Kočický, 2012)

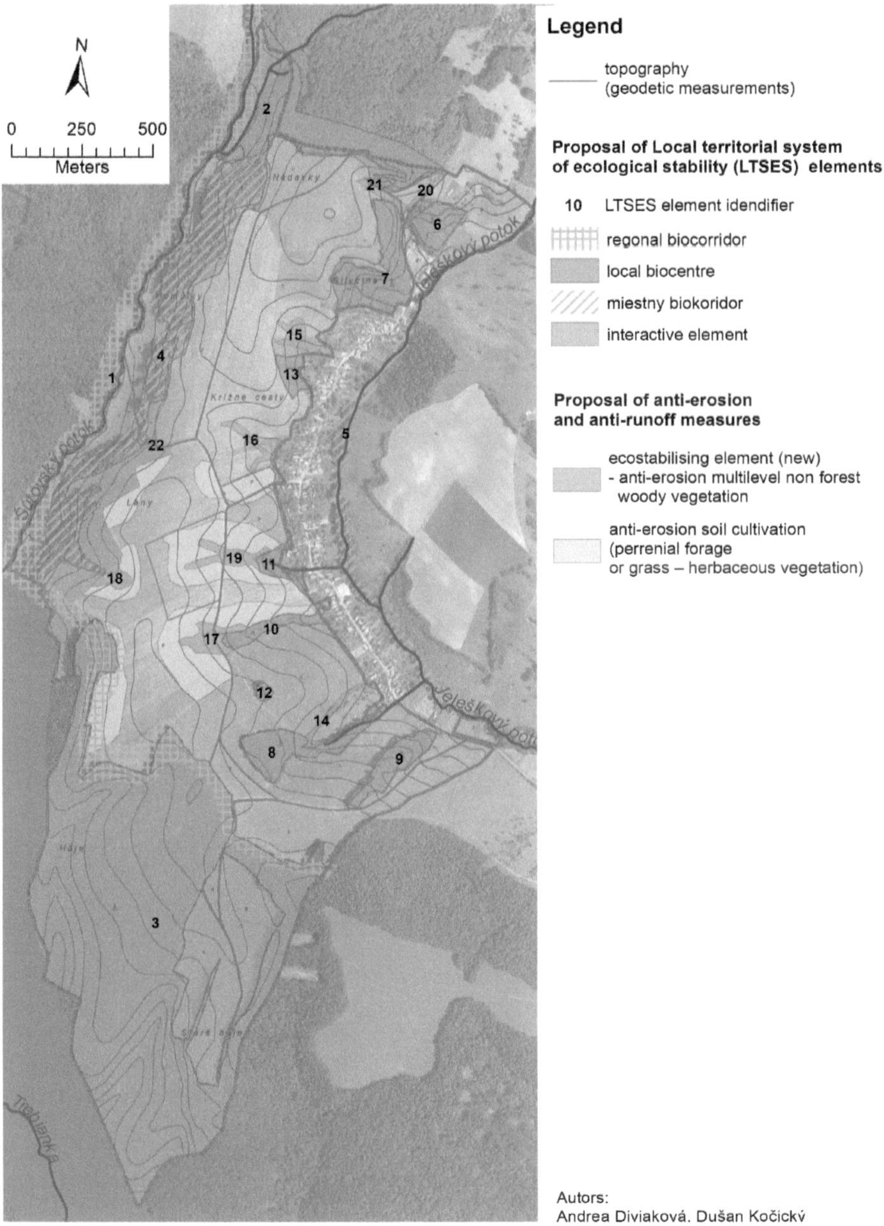

Fig. 30: TSES Proposal (Diviaková, Kočický, 2012 in Diviaková, Kočický, Novikmec, Svitok, 2012)

Annexes

Annex 1

Measure	National environmental legislation	EU legislation	
No. 1. Investment in agricultural enterprises	Act No. 138/1973 Coll. On water (Water Act) Act No. 307/1992 Coll. On the protection of agricultural land Act No. 127/1994 Coll. On EIA	85/337/EEC (97/11/EC)-EIA 91/676/EEC-nitrates 96/61/EC-IPPC 91/156/EEC - waste 96/62/EC - air 93/389/EEC - greenhouse gases	
No. 2. Improvement of processing and marketing of agricultural products	Act No. 127/1994 Coll. On EIA Act No. 138/1973 Coll. On water (Water Act) Act No. 224/1998 on ecological and biofood production	91/676/EEC-nitrates 91/156/EEC - waste 880/92/EEC on ecological EC Regulation No. 2092/1991	
No. 3. Support of establishment of producer groups			
No. 4. Diversification activities in rural areas	Act No. 61/1997 on forests, as amended Act No. 100/1997 Coll. On management of forests and on state administration in forestry Act No. 50/1976 Coll. (Building Act) as amended	85/337/EEC (97/11/EC)-EIA	Resolution of the Government of the Slovak Republic No. 222/1997 on the Programme of renewal of villages in Slovakia
No. 5. Forestry	Act No. 61/1997 on forests, as amended Act No. 100/1997 Coll. On management of forests and on state administration in forestry Act No. 287/1994 on landscape protection	92/43/EEC- habitats and species 79/409/EEC - birds	World Culture and Natural heritage Protection Biological Diversity Convention Convention of migratory species and animals convention on the conservation of European wildlife and Natural Habitats

No. 6. Agricultural production methods designed to protect the environment and maintain countryside	Act No. 138/1973 on waters Act No. 287/1994 on natural and landscape protection Act No. 224/1998 on environmentally-friendly agriculture and the production of biofood	92/43/EEC - habitats and species 79/409/EEC - birds 91/676/EEC - nitrates	territorial systems of ecological stability Ramsar convention World Culture and Natural heritage Protection Biological Diversity Convention Convention of migratory species and animals convention on the conservation of European wildlife and Natural Habitats
No. 7. Land consolidation	Act No. 287/1994 on natural and landscape Protection Act No. 330/91 on land consolidation		territorial systems of ecological stability at local level
No. 8. Development of human resources	Act No. 171/1998 on information access	85/337/EEC (97/11/EC) - EIA 96/61/EC - IPPC	
No. 9. Technical assistance	Act No. 50/1976 Coll. (The building Act) as amended Act No. 287/1994 on natural and landscape protection	91/271/EEC - urban waste water 91/156/EEC - waste 91/689/EEC - hazardous waste	Resolution of the Government of the Slovak Republic No. 222/1997 on the Programme of renewal of villages in Slovakia territorial systems of ecological stability at regional and local levels

Further details on EU policies and legislation procedures can be found in Annex VI of the SAPARD Plan (Acqui implementation in environmental legislation)

Annex 2: Environmental correspondence between the general and specific objectives of the SAPARD Plan

General objectives **Specific Objectives**	**1.** To help the creation of competitive agrifood sector, capable of full integration and operation in the EU area in a developed multifunctional agriculture.	**2.** The improvement the quality of life of rural population, provision of a sufficient number of jobs and adequate income even for agricultural less favoured regions (need for ecological approach and sustainable development of rural areas).
Priority No. 1		
1. By supporting investment in technologies, to achieve restructuring and enhance efficiency in agricultural production	+++	
2. To ensure further development of individual branches of the food industry with conditions valid in EU	+++	++
3. To support the establishment, formation and simplification of administrative operations for producer groups	++	+
Priority No. 2		
4. Preserve and improve the balance of economic opportunity and social conditions for the rural population	+++	+++
5. Development of economic and environmental functions of forest management in rural areas	++	+++
6. To acquire sufficient experience to be able to prepare agri-environmental programme and to deliver management training through five pilot projects	+++	+++
7. Development and implementation of land consolidation projects	+	+++
Priority No. 3		
8. To provide farmers with and others with necessary skill by training in different spheres relevant to agricultural and rural development	+++	+++
9. To support the process of alignment of the farming sector and rural areas, interactive programming and planning including territorial planning and preparation of studies for farmers and rural areas	+++	+++

Level of correspondence: +++: High ++: Medium +: Low

Annex 3

1. Correspondence between the specific objectives and the measures of Priority 1

Specific Objectives / **Measures**	**1.** By supporting investment in technologies, to achieve restructuring and enhance efficiency in agricultural production	**2.** To ensure further development of individual branches of the food industry with conditions valid in EU	**3.** To support the establishment, formation and simplification of administrative operations for producer groups
Measure 1	+++	++	
Measure 2	+++	+++	+++
Measure 3	+	++	+++

2. Correspondence between the specific objectives and the measures of Priority 2

Specific Objectives / **Measures**	1. Preserve and improve the balance of economic opportunity and social conditions for the rural population	**2.** Development of economic and environmental functions of forest management in rural areas	**3.** To acquire sufficient experience to be able to prepare agri-environmental programme and to deliver management training through five pilot projects	**4.** Development and implementation of land consolidation projects
Measure 4	+++	+		
Measure 5		+++		
Measure 6			+++	++
Measure 7	+++	+	+	+++

3. Correspondence between the specific objectives and the measures of Priority 3

Specific Objectives / **Measures**	**1.** To provide farmers with and others with necessary skill by training in different spheres relevant to agricultural and rural development	**2.** To support the process of alignment of the farming sector and rural areas, interactive programming and planning including territorial planning and preparation of studies for farmers and rural areas
Measure 8	+++	
Measure 9		+++

Level of correspondence: +++: High ++: Medium +: Low

Annex 4

Measure	**Monitoring Indicators**	
Priority No. 1	**Qualitative**	**Quantitative**
Measure No. 1: Investment in agricultural enterprises	water, air and soil emission indicators	
Measure No. 2: Improvement of processing and marketing of agricultural products	environmental conditions for foodstuff production	
Measure No. 3: Support of establishment of producer groups		
Priority No. 2		
Measure No. 4: Diversification activities in rural areas	reconstruction of valuable areas - landscape features, historical parks	
Measure No. 5: Forestry	reduction of environmental impact soil erosion (tractors), greenhouse gases water quality, water quantity	No. of project investments in forest nurseries
Measure No. 6: Agricultural production methods designed to protect the environment and maintain the countryside	protection of natural heritage protection of cultural heritage agri-environmental schemes interest of farmers in agro-environmental schemes	% of farmers who would like to continue with agro-envir. Schemes net land surface under environmentally friendly agricultural practices (% in total arable land)
Measure No. 7: Land consolidation	landscape protection - territorial system of ecological stability revitalisation of landscape	number of revitalisation projects
Priority No. 3		
Measure No. 8: Development of human resources	training in environmentally friendly methods of farming	% of trained
Measure No. 9: Technical assistance	technical infrastructure projects drinking water distribution network sewage network, liquid waste treatment facilities waste disposal sites	number of such projects

Bibliography

Agenda 21 a ukazovatele trvalo udržateľného rozvoja, 1996: MŽP SR, Bratislava, 520pp.

Belčáková, I., 1995: SEA and spatial planning in Slovakia, IXth Seminar of the Project Methodology, Focalisation, Evaluation and Scope of EIA. NATO-CCMS, Lanaken, Belgium, 20–24 September.

Belčáková, I., 2000: Agriculture and rural development plan of the Slovak Republic over the 2000–2006 period - Prior appraisal - Environmental part, EIA Centre at Faculty of Architecture STU, Bratislava, 15pp. + annexes.

Belčáková, I., 2001: New trends of SEA in spatial planning. PhD thesis (in Slovak), Faculty of Natural Sciences, Comenius University in Bratislava, 127pp.

Belčáková, I., 2008: Report preparation and impact assessment methods and techniques. In: Fischer, T.B., Gazzola, P., Jha-Thakur, U., Belčáková, I., Aschemann, A. (eds.): Environmental Assessment Lecturer's Handbook. ROAD, Bratislava, pp. 157–156.

Belčáková, I., 2012: Landscape planning framework on the environmental assessment - linkages and mutual benefits. Ekológia/Ecology, vol. 31, no. 1, pp. 1–11.

Belčáková, I., 2015: Hodnotenie vplyvov na krajinu v plánovacom procese. 1. vyd. Veda, Bratislava, 136 s.

Belčáková, I., 2016: Strategic environmental assessment - An instrument for better decision-making towards urban sustainable planning. Procedia Engineering, vol. 161, pp. 2058–2061.

Belčáková, I., Finka, M., 1996a: Metodika k implemenetácii § 35 zákona NR SR č. 127/1994 Z.z. na hodnotenie územnoplánovacej dokumentácii (Methodology to Implementation of Environmental Assessment on Spatial Planning Documentation in the Slovak Republic of §35 of the EIA Act No. 127/1994), manuscript. FA STU, Bratislava.

Belčáková, I., Finka, M., 1996b: Perspektívy strategického hodnotenia vplyvov na životné prostredie na Slovensku (Perspectives of strategic environmental assessment in spatial planning in Slovakia), Životné prostredie, vol. XXX, no. 1, pp. 31–33.

Belčáková, I., Finka, M., 1999: Environmentálne hodnotenie územnoplánovacej dokumentácie (Environmental assesment of spatial planning documentation), Životné prostredie, vol. 33, no. 4, pp. 206–210.

Belčáková, I., Finka, M., 2000: Strategic environmental assessment of land use/spatial plans in EU and SR. In: Gal, P., Belcakova, I. (eds.): Current Legislation and Standards of Spatial Planning in Social Transformation and European Integration. FA STU, Bratislava, pp. 257–264.

Belčáková, I., Petríková, D., 2003: Environmentálne plánovanie. FA STU, Bratislava, 79pp.

Belčáková, I., Nelson, P., 2006: SEA in Spatial Planning. In International Experience and Perspectives in SEA: A Global Conference on Strategic Environmental Assessment, 26–30 September 2005. Session C4. Česká zemědělská univerzita, Praha, 66pp. Available at: http://www.iaia.org/pdf/ConferenceDocuments/SEA-Prague/05%20 SEA%20final%20program.pdf.

Benett, G., 1991: Towards a European Ecological Network. Institute for European Environmental Policy, Arnhem, 80pp.

Brodniansky, B. Machlica, J., 2012: Hluková štúdia "Horská osada Vrátna – Tižinka", vplyv mobilných a stacionárnych zdrojov hluku dopravy na vonkajšie prostredie. Inžinierske stavby spol. s.r.o., Martin, 9 s.

Brown, A., Therivel, R., 2000: 'Principles to guide the development of strategic environmental assessment methodology.' Impact Assessment and Project Appraisal, vol. 18, pp. 183–189.

Buček, A., Lacina, J., 1995: Přírodovědná východiska ÚSES. In: Löw, J., Buček, A., Lacina, J., Míchal, I., Plos, J., Petříček, V. (eds.): Rukověť projektanta místního ÚSES. Doplněk, Brno, pp. 9–28.

Buček, A., Lacina, J.,1984: Biogeografický přístup k vytváření územních systému ekologické stability krajiny. Zprávy Geografického ústavu ČSAV Brno, vol. 21, no. 4, pp. 27–35.

Buček, A., Lacina, J., Löw, J., 1984: Teoretické východiská a typológia ÚSES. Pracovné materiály KRB. Agroprojekt Brno, 12pp.

Canter, L., Sadler, B.,1997: A Tool Kit for Effective EIA Practice – Review of Methods and Perspectives on their Application. A Supplementary Report of the International Study of the Effectiveness of Environmental Assessment. Environmental and Ground Water Institute, University of Oklahoma, Norman, OK.

Cherp, A., 2001: SEA in newly independent states. In: Dusik, J. (ed.): Proceedings of International Workshop on Public Participation and Health Aspects in Strategic Environmental Assessment. Regional Environmental Center for Central and Eastern Europe, Szentendre.

Commission of the European Communities – DGXI, 1998: Case studies on SEA.

CSIR, 1996: Strategic Environmental Assessment – A Primer. CSIR, Stellenbosch.

Council of Europe, 2000: European Landscape Convention. European Treaty Series No. 176. Council of Europe, Florence.

Curran, J.M., Wood, C.M., Hilton, M., 1998: 'Environmental appraisal of UK development plans: Current practice and future directions.' Environmental and Planning B: Planning and Design, vol. 25, pp. 411–433.

Dalal-Clayton, B., Sadler, B., 2005: Strategic Environmental Assessment – A Sourcebook and Reference Guide to International Experience. Eartscan, London.

Demianová, V., 1985: Prieskum intenzity erózie pôdy na vybraných trasách turistických chodníkov v CHKO Malá Fatra vo vzťahu k frekvencii návštevníkov. Obdobie riešenia 1983-1986. Dielčia správa. ÚŠOP – Správa CHKO Malá Fatra, Gbeľany, 16 s.

DETR, 1998: Strategic Environmental Appraisal. Report of the International Seminar on SEA, Lincoln, 27–29 May. Department of Environment, Transport and the Regions, London, 35pp.

Diviaková, A., Kočický, D., Novikmec, M., Svitok, M., 2012: Miestny územný systém ekologickej stability pre project pozemkových úprav. Zvolen, k.ú. Kocúrany, 65pp. + pictures.

Eggenberger, M., Partidario, M.R., 2000: Development of a framework to assist the integration of environmental, social and economic issues in planning. Impact Assessment and Project Appraisal, vol. 18, no. 3, pp. 201–207.

Elling, B. 2000: Integration of strategic environmental asssesment into regional spatial planning. Project Appraisal, vol. 18, no. 3, pp. 233–243.

European Commission (EC), 2001: Directive 2001/42/EC of the European Parliament and of the Council of 27 June 2001 on the assessment of the effects of certain plans and programmes on the environment. Official Journal of the European Communities, No. L.197, pp. 30–37.

European Commission (EC), 2014: Directive 2014/52/EU of the European Parliament and of the Council of 16 April 2014 amending Directive 2011/92/EU on the assessment of the effects of certain public and private projects on the environment. Official Journal of the European Union, No. L 124/1.

EU Compendium of Spatial Planning Systems and Policies, CEC, 1997.

European Landscape Convention, 2000: Council of Europe, 20th October, 2000. Florence.

European Regional Spatial Planning Charter, CoE, 1983.

Finka, M., Belčáková, I., 1997: Návrh zásad vykonávacej vyhlášky pre implementáciu casti §35 Zákona NR SR c. 127/1994 Z.z. o posudzovaní vplyvov na životné prostredie, venovanej hodnoteniu ÚPD (Proposal of Executive Regulation Principles for §35 of EIA Act). Centrum EIA Slovakia, Bratislava.

Fischer, T.B., 2002: SEA approaches and tools - requirements of tiered planning systems. In: Marsden, S., Dovers, S (eds.): Strategic Environmental Assessment in Australasia. The Federation Press, Annandale, NSW, pp. 99–113.

Fischer, T.B., 2006: IAIA Conference on "International Experience and perspectives in SEA", 26-30 September, 2005, Prague, Czech Republic: Conclusions Stream C: Linkages between SEA and other assessment or planning tools. Journal of Environmental Assessment Policy and Management, vol. 8, no. 4, pp. 495–504.

Fischer, T.B., 2007: Theory and Practice of Strategic Environmental Assessment. Earthscan, London.

Flajs, T., 2012: Záverečná správa k mapovaniu vtáctva a obojživelníkov na lokalite Vrátna dolina - Tižinka. 6 s.

Formann, R.T.T., Godron, M., 1986: Landscape Ecology. Wiley, New York, p. 595.

Forman, R.T.T., Godron, M., 1993: Krajinná ekologie. Academia, Praha, p. 584.

Haaren, v C., Galler, C., Ott, S., 2008. Landscape Planning. The Basis of Sustainable Landscape Development. Federal Agency for Nature Conservation, Field Office Leipzig, Lepzig.

Haase, G., Hubrich, H., Schluter, H., Mannsfeld, K., Kugler, H., Richter, H., Barsch, H., Kopp, D., Schwanecke, W., 1974: Erfassung, Kartierung und Kennzeichnung von Naturraumtypen. Interpretation von Naturraumpotentialen und Ermittlung von Bewertungsmoglichkeiten fuer volkswirtschaftlich bedeutsame Formen der Flächennutzung. Geographisches Institut der AdW der DDR, Bericht, Leipzig.

Hamza, J., 2012: Rozpylová štúdia 436/2012. Horská osada Tižinka. Inžinierske stavby spol. s.r.o., Martin, 11 s.

Hanski I., 1998: Metapopulation dynamics. Nature, vol. 396, pp. 41–49.

Herberg, A., 2000: Umwelt und Landschaftsplanung in den Ländern der EU und der Schweiz. Arbeitsmaterialien zur Landschaftsplanung, Heft 15 (CD-ROM), Technische Universität Berlin.

Hlôška, L., 2012: Aktuálne rozšírenie a početnosť vybraných druhov drobných zemných cicavcov (Rodentia, Soricimorpha) v lokalite Tižinka (NP Malá Fatra, CHVÚ Malá Fatra). Považské múzeum, Žilina, 20 s.

Hrnčiarová, T. et al., 1997: Ekologická únosnosť krajiny: metodika a aplikácia na 3 benefičné územia. I–IV. časť. Ekologický projekt MŽP SR. ÚKE SAV, Bratislava, 490 s. (nepubl.).

Hrnčiarová, T., Izakovičová, Z., 2000: Environmental Approaches to Sustainable Development. Združenie KRAJINA 21, Bratislava, 252pp.

ICON - IC Consultants Ltd., 2001: SEA and Integration of the Environment into Strategic Decision-Making. European Commission, Brussels.

Ihnatišinová, K., Remenec, V., Ridoško, Š., 2011, 2012: Súhrnná technická správa stavby - Horská osada (Rodinná chata - typ 01, Rodinná chata - typ 02, Apartmánový dom - typ 01, Apartmánový dom - typ 02, Apartmánový dom - typ 03, Apartmánový dom - typ 04) + výkresy, Optima Finance, s.r.o.

Izakovičová, Z., 2000: Landscape planning - a main landscape-ecological regulation for territorial development. In: Gál, P., Belčáková, I. (eds.): Nástroje priestorového plánovania v kontexte transformácie a európskej integrácie. Slovenská technická univerzita, Bratislava pp. 242–248.

Izakovičová, Z., Izakovičová, Z., Hrnčiarová, T., Králik, J., Liška, M., Miklós, L., Moyzeová, M., Pauditšová, E., Ružičková, H., Šíbl, J., Tremboš, P., 2000: Metodické pokyny na vypracovanie projektov regionálnych územných systémov ekologickej stability a miestnych územných systémov ekologickej stability. MŽP SR, Združenie KRAJINA 21, Bratislava, 155pp.

Izakovičová, Z., 2012: Landscape-ecological plan as the basic tool for sustainable land use, GeoScape, vol. 7, no. 1, pp. 8–17.

João, E., 2005: SEA outlook - future challenges and possibilities. In: Schmidt, M., João, E., Albrecht, E.I. (eds.): Implementing Strategic Environmental Assessment. Springer Verlag, pp. 691–700.

Jones, C., Baker, M., Carter, J., Jay, S., Short, M., Wood, C. (eds.) 2005: Strategic Environmental Assessment and Land Use Planning. London, Earthscan.

Jongman, R.H.G., 1995: Nature conservation planning in Europe: Developing ecological networks. Landscape Urban Planning, vol. 32, pp. 169–183.

Jurko, A., 1986: Krajinnoekologická významnosť rastlinných spoločenstiev. In: Ekologická optimalizácia využívania Východoslovenskej nížiny. III. diel. ÚEBE SAV - Slovosivo, Michalovce, pp. 214–218.

Jurko, A., 1990: Ekologické a socioekonomické hodnotenie vegetácie. Príroda, Bratislava, 195pp.

Klees, R., Capcelea, A., Barannik, A., 2002: Environmental Impact Assesment (EIA) Systems in Europe and Central Asia Countries. the Worldbank, Washington, DC.

Kleinschmidt, V., Wagner, D., 1998: Strategic Environmental Assessment in Europe. Fourth European Workshop on EIA. Kluwer Academic Publisher, Dordrecht.

Kočická, E., 2004: Stanovenie ekologickej únosnosti na základe hodnotenia citlivosti krajiny na acidifikáciu (modelové územie povodie Belianskeho potoka - Štiavnické vrchy). Dizertačná práca. Katedra UNESCO, FEE TU Zvolen, Zvolen, 124 s. + prílohy (nepubl.).

Kočická, E., Nikolov, C.H., Brodniansky, B., Hamza, J., Hlôška, L., Ihnatišinová, K., Ridoško, Š., 2012: Horská osada Tižinka. Správa o hodnotení. 150 s. + prílohy.

Kristiník, S., Pekara, J., Kollár, K., Kučerová, M., 2010: Územný plán sídelného útvaru Terchová, Zmena a doplnok č. 2. PROKRIST, Žilina.

Kružliaková, E., 2012: Monitoring návštevnosti 2012 (záverečná správa č.j. NPMF/2012/2). Interné materiály Správy NP Malá Fatra, ŠOP SR, 14 s.

Lee, N. and Walsh, F., 1992: 'Strategic environmental assessment: An overview.' Project Appraisal, vol. 7, pp. 126-136.

Lee N. and Hughes J., 1995: Strategic environmental assessment, legislation and procedures in the community, final report. EIA Centre, University of Manchester, Manchester.

Löw, J., Buček, A., Lacina, J., Míchal, I., Plos, J., Petříček, V., 1995: Rukověť projektanta místního ÚSES. Doplněk, Brno, 124pp.

Mac Arthur, R.H., Wilson, E.D., 1967: The Theory of Island Biogeography. Princeton University Press, Princeton, New York, 233pp.

Míchal, I., 1992: Ekologická stabilita. Veronica, Brno, 244pp.

Miklós, L., 1979: Landscape optimalization - Subject and aim of the methodics of landscape biological planning. In: Collection of papers for Vth International Symposium on Problems of Ecological Landscape Research, Stará Lesná - High Tatras, CSSR, pp. 493-503.

Miklós, L., 1986: Stabilita krajiny v ekologickom genereli SSR. Životné prostredie, vol. 20, no. 2, pp. 87-93.

Miklós, L., 1991: Zásady slovenskej ekologickej politiky. Životné prostredie, vol. 25, no. 4, pp. 174-178.

Miklós, L., 1992: Ekologizácia priestorovej organizácie, využitia a ochrany krajiny. Slovenská technická knižnica, Bratislava, 101 s.

Miklós, L., 1995: Landscape-ecological Aspects of the Organisation and Planning of Space. Universität für Bodenkultur Wien, 91pp.

Miklós, L., 1996: The concept of the territorial system of ecological stability in Slovakia. In: Jongmann, R.H.G. (ed.): Ecological and Landscape Consequences of Land-use Change in Europe. ECNC Publication Series on Man and Nature 2, Tilburg, pp. 385-406.

Miklós, L., Diviaková, A., Izakovičová, Z., 2011: Ekologické siete a územné systémy ekologickej stability. Vydavateľstvo TU vo Zvolene, Zvolen, 141 s.

Miklós, L., Hrnčiarová, T. (eds.), 2002: Atlas krajiny Slovenskej republiky [Landscape Atlas of the Slovak Republic]. 1. vyd. MŽP SR, Bratislava, 344 s.

Miklós, L., Izakovičová, Z., 1997: Krajina ako geosystém. VEDA, Bratislava, 152 s.

Miklós, L., Izakovičová Z., 2007: Management of landscape changes in Slovakia. In: Bunce, R.G.H., Jongman, R.H.G., Hojas, L., Weiil, S. (eds.): 25 Years of Landscape Ecology: Scientific Principles in Practice. Proceeding from the 7th IALE World Congress - 2. Part. IALE, Wageningen, the Netherlands, pp. 801–802.

Miklós, L., Kočická, E., Kočický, D., Diviaková, A., 2015: Geosystémy ako krajinnoekologická základňa pre integrovaný manažment krajiny. Technická univerzita vo Zvolene, Zvolene, 101 s. + prílohy.

Miklós, L., Kozová, M., Ružička, M. (eds), 1986: Ekologický plán využívania Východoslovenskej nížiny v mierke 1:25 000. In: Ekologická optimalizácia využívania VSN. ÚEBE SAV, Bratislava, pp. 5–312.

Miklós, L., Špinerová, A., 2011: Krajinno-ekologické plánovanie LANDEP [The Landscape - Ecological Planning LANDEP. In Slovak]. Vojenský kartografický ústav, Harmanec, 158pp.

MŽP SR, 1993: Metodické pokyny na spracovanie územných systémov ekologickej stability. Ministerstvo životného prostredia SR, Bratislava.

Mörtberg, U.M., Balfors, B., Knol, W.C., 2007: Landscape ecological assessment: A tool for integrating biodiversity issues in strategic environmental assessment and planning. Journal of Environmental Management, vol. 82, pp. 457–470.

Opdam P., Foppen R., Reijnen R., Schotman A., 1995: The landscape ecological approach in bird conservation: Integrating the metapopulation concept into spatial planning. Ibis, vol. 137, pp. 139–146.

Owens, S., Cowell, R., 2002: Land and Limits: Interpreting Sustainability in the Planning Process. Routlege, London.

Partidário, M.R., 1999: Strategic Environmental Assessment - A Course Manual, SEA Pre-Meeting Training Course, IAIA´99 (non-published).

Partidário, M.R., 2000: Integration of environmental, social and economic issues in planning and how this can be used in SEA (in Slovak). In: Nástroje priestorového plánovania v kontexte trannsformácie a európslek integrácie. FA STU, Bratislava, pp. 118–128.

Partidário, M.R., 2004: The contribution of strategic impact assessment to planning evaluation. In: Miller, D., Patassini, D. (eds.): Accounting for Non-market Values in Planning Evaluation. Aldershot: Ashgate Publ.

Partidário, M.R., Clark, R. (eds.), 2000: Perspectives on Strategic Environmental. Assessment Lewis Publishers/CRC Press, Boca Raton, FL.

Pauditšová, E., Reháčková, T., Ružičková, J., 2007: Metodický návod na vypracovanie miestneho územného systému ekologickej stability. Acta Environmentalica Universitatis Comenianae, vol.15, no. 2, pp. 61–82.

Piscová, V., Kanka, R., Krajčí, J., Barančok, P., 2011: Short-term trampling experiments in the Juncetum trifidi Krajina 1933 Association. Ekológia (Bratislava), vol. 30, no. 3, pp. 322–333. DOI: 10.4149/ekol-2011-03-322.

Platzer ,U., 2000: Strategic environmental assessment. Report of the Workshop in Semering, Austria, October 1998.

Roberts, J.A., 1991: Just What is EIR. Global Environmental Management Services, Sacramento, 209 s.

Ruzicka, M., Miklós, L., 1979: Teoretické a metodologické základy biologického planovania krajiny. Záverecná správa úlohy VI-3-5/1. ÚEBE SAV, Bratislava, 221pp.

Ružička, M., Miklós, L., 1982a: Metodické poznatky ekologického hodnotenia územia pre zónu a sídelný útvar (na príklade Rimavskej Soboty). ActaEcologica, vol. 9, no. 26, 74pp.

Ružička, M., Miklós, L., 1982b: Landscape-ecological planning (LANDEP) in the process of territorial planning. Ekológia (ČSSR), vol. 1, pp. 297–312.

Ružička, M., Miklós, L., 1990: Basic premises and methods in landscape-ecological planning and optimisation. In: Zonnenveld, I.S., Forman, R.T.T. (eds.): Changing Landscapes: An Ecological Perspectives. Springer Verlag, New York, pp. 233–260.

Sadler, B., Verheem, R., (eds.), 1996: Strategic environmental assesment. Status, Challenges and Future Directions, Publication No. 53. Ministry of Housing, Spatial Planning and the Environment, The Hague.

Sadler, B., 2001a: Strategic environmental assessment: An aide memoire to drafting a SEA protocol to the Espoo Convention. In: Dusik, J. (ed.): Proceedings of International Workshop on Public Participation and Health Aspects in Strategic Environmental Assessment. Regional Environmental Center for Central and Eastern Europe, Szentendre.

Sadler, B., 2001b: A framework approach to strategic environmental assessment: Aims, principles and elements of good practice. In: Dusik, J. (ed.): Proceedings of International Workshop on Public Participation and Health Aspects in Strategic Environmental Assessment. Regional Environmental Center for Central and Eastern Europe, Szentendre.

Sheate, W.R., Byron, H.J., Smith, S.P., 2004: Implementing the SEA directive: sectoral challenges and opportunities for the UK and EU. European Environment, vol. 14, pp. 73–93.

Schmidt, M., Joao, E., Albrecht, E. (eds.), 2004: Implementing Strategic Environmental Assessment. Springer, Berlin, Heidelberg, 234pp.

Sibilová, L., 2009: Monitoring návštevnosti 2009 (záverečná správa č. j. NPMF/1013/2009/2). Správa NP Malá Fatra, ŠOP SR, 9 s.

Smit, B., Spalding, H., 1995: Methods for cumulative effects assessment. Environmental Impact Assessment Review, vol. 15, pp. 81–106.

Stanová, V., Valachovič, M. (eds.), 2002: Katalóg biotopov Slovenska. DAPHNE – Inštitút aplikovanej ekológie, Bratislava, 225 s.

Thérivel, R., Wilson, E., Thompson, S., Heany, D., Pritchard, D., 1992: Strategic Enviornmental Assessment. Earthscan, London.

Thérivel, R., 2004: Strategic Environmental Assessment in Action. Earthscan, London.

Thérivel, R., Partdário, M.R. (eds.), 1996: The Practice of Strategic Environmental Assessment. Earthscan, London.

United Nations Economic Commission for Europe (UN ECE), 1998: Convention on Access to Information, Public Participation on Decision-Making and Access to Justice in Environmental Matters, Aarhus Convention. UN ECE, Geneva.

United Nations Economic Commission for Europe (UN ECE), 2003: Protocol on Strategic Environmental Assessment to the Convention on Environmental Impact Assessment in a Transboundary Context. Available at:

https://www.unece.org/fileadmin/DAM/env/eia/documents/legaltexts/protocolenglish.pdf (accessed August, 2018).

Verheem, R., 1992: Environmental assessment at strategic levels in the Netherlands. Project Appraisal, vol. 7, pp. 150–156.

Westman, W.E., 1985: Ecology, Impact Assessment and Environmental Planning.Wiley, New York, pp. 158.

Wiggering, D., Glemnitz, H., Muller, S., Stachow, Z., 2007: Indicators for multifunctionality impacts in landscape. In: Bunce, R.G.H., Jongman, R.H.G., Hojas, L., Weiil, S. (eds.): Scientific Principles in Practice. Proceedings from the 7th IALE World Congress – 2. Part.. IALE, Wageningen, the Netherlands, pp. 817–818.

Wood, C.M., Dejeddour, M., 1989: 'The environmental assessment of policies, plans and programmes,' Volume 1 of Interim Report to the European Commission on Environmental Assessment of Policies, Plans. EIA Centre at University of Manchester, Manchester.

Wood, C.M., Dejeddour, M., 1992: Strategic environmental assessment: EA of policies, plans and programmes. Impact Assessment Bulletin, vol. 10, pp. 3–22.

About Authors

Ingrid Belčáková is an Associate Professor in Environmental Planning and Management at Technical University in Zvolen, Faculty of Ecology and Environmental Sciences. She has been active in environmental planning and management for more than 20 years, as a researcher, practitioner and trainer. An important part of her academic output is landscape assessment and land use planning resulting in a number of articles and books.

László Miklós is a Professor in Environmental Management at Technical University in Zvolen, Faculty of Ecology and Environmental Sciences and Head of UNESCO-Chair for sustainable development and ecological awareness. In the past he was a Minister for the Environment of the Slovak Republic. He has over 40 years of research and practical experience with environmental management in an international context. He has published widely on the topic and is author of many books.

Anna Špinerová is a senior lecturer at UNESCO-Chair for sustainable development and ecological awareness. She is a co-author of many books and articles in the field of landscape ecological planning. She frequently presents her practical and research experience at both national and international conferences.

Andrea Diviaková is a senior lecturer at Technical University in Zvolen, Faculty of Ecology and Environmental Sciences, UNESCO Department. She has a lot of educational skills, her main interest is in the fields of ecological networks (TSES), nature and landscape protection, ecological landscape stability.

Erika Kočická is a research assistant at Technical University in Zvolen, Faculty of Ecology and Environmental Sciences, UNESCO Department. She has participated in several projects in field of optimalisation of landscape structure, EIA/SEA), landscape carrying capacity, etc. as a team leader, manager and co-manager.

Eliška Belaňová is landscape ecologist. She has finished her PhD studies in 2014 at Technical University in Zvolen, Faculty of Ecology and Environmental Sciences, UNESCO Department. Since then she has been active in both lecturing and research activities in the fields of landscape plannng and integrated landscape management.

www.ingramcontent.com/pod-product-compliance
Ingram Content Group UK Ltd.
Pitfield, Milton Keynes, MK11 3LW, UK
UKHW041839031026
15587UKWH00002B/876

9 783631 749715